The Rose Metal Press Field Guide to
PROSE POETRY

THE ROSE METAL PRESS

Field Guide to
Prose Poetry

Contemporary Poets
in Discussion and Practice

Edited by Gary L. McDowell
and F. Daniel Rzicznek

Rose Metal Press

2010

Acknowledgments for previously published works appear on page 185, which constitutes an extension of the copyright page.

Rose Metal Press, Inc.
P.O. Box 1956
Brookline, MA 02446
rosemetalpress@gmail.com
www.rosemetalpress.com

Library of Congress Control Number: 2010922802

ISBN: 978-0-9789848-8-5

Cover and interior design by Rebecca Saraceno
Cover typefaces: Avenir and Utopia; Interior typefaces: Utopia, with Avenir
See "A Note About the Type" for more information about the type.

This book is manufactured in the United States of America and printed on acid-free paper.

Funding for this book was given in loving memory of Marie T. Maixner (1918-2008).

  This book was supported in part by grants from the National Endowment for the Arts and the Massachusetts Cultural Council.

For our teachers

TABLE OF CONTENTS

Field Notes: A Preface XI
Rebellion Still Has Its Attractions: A Case for Prose Poetry XV

1 – Prose Poem Essay on the Prose Poem
Bob Hicok

ON DISCOVERY: VERSE THAT IS NOT PROSE, PROSE THAT IS NOT VERSE

3 – Right Margin Man(ifesto): This Is How I Mean
Encouragement for a Man Falling to His Death, Personality Quiz
Christopher Kennedy

7 – "Goodtime Jesus" and Other Sort-of Prose Poems
Union Station, Los Angeles (The Reagan Years), Harvest News
James Harms

14 – Discovering the Prose Poem in Norfolk, Virginia
Paint, Hotel
David Daniel

19 – Enchiladas for the Stolen Boys: A Personal History
of the Prose Poem
Love Crushed Us with Its Big Death Truck, Signs of Life
Andrew Michael Roberts

25 – Happy (Or How It Took Me Twenty Years to Almost
"Get" the Prose Poem)
Embarazar, Napping on the Afternoon of My 39th Birthday
Denise Duhamel

ON INFLUENCE: REVELATION AND REVOLUTION

31 – I Cannot Escape the Prose Poem
(How to Sink the Surface), (After Contemplating Wintering
in Water)
Brigitte Byrd

36 – The Ocean Outside the Door: A Few Transformations
Brought to You By the Prose Poem Laboratory
The Experiment, Many Worlds
Jeffrey Skinner

41 – **Something Like a Meditation**
Meditation on a Suicide, Noise
Alexander Long

48 – **Why I Write Prose Poems**
October Again, Wish
Kathleen McGookey

52 – **A Wolf in Grandma's Clothes: Undressing the Prose Poem**
Still Life with Steam Engine, Still Life with Gravestone
Michael Robins

ON DEFINITION: CATALOGING THE NEW BEASTS

56 – **No Easy Out: Some Definitions of the Prose Poem**
I stood too close…, I was a fabulous…
David Keplinger

60 – **Thankfully, Philip Larkin Will Never Read This**
Furnace, National Poetry Month
Kevin Griffith

64 – **Crashing the Party: Going Home with the Prose Poem You Want**
I Wish I Were Mexico, He Said Discipline Is the Highest Form of Love
Beckian Fritz Goldberg

69 – **Ticking the Box: The Rules and Permissions of the Prose Poem Form**
ORD, On the Use of a View: An Essay
Arielle Greenberg

74 – **Split: Seam and Abyss in the Prose Poem**
from Party in My Body
Mark Wallace

ON THEORY: NO MATTER WHAT YOU CALL IT

79 – **Prose Poem Electric**
Soup for an Oligarch, the other word for thesaurus
Maurice Kilwein Guevara

85 – **Paragraphic Verses**
The Day After the Day of the Dead, Voice Road
William Olsen

91 – The Poem in the Gray Flannel Suit
   Dear Editor 18 January, Dear Editor 30 October
   Amy Newman

99 – Out of My Prose Poem Past: Using the Prose Poem to Enter
   the Language of Films Noir
   Good Idea, The Dark Lady of the Movies
   David Lazar

104 – Blockheads and Stanzagraphers
   Schism, You Know What They Say about Pears
   Robert Miltner

ON CRAFT: THE MUSIC OF THE SENTENCE

112 – The Unbroken Line
   The earth submits to seasonal drift…, I couldn't find
   the mushrooms…
   Gary Young

115 – Just Running: Open Landscape and the Prose Poem
   I Finde in a Boke Compiled to this Matere an Olde Histoire,
   Photograph of a Young Girl, 1941
   Nancy Eimers

121 – Hyphen: Sketching the Bridge with Invisible Ink
   from Installations, After Serving
   Joe Bonomo

127 – A Carnival Comes to Town: Showing Prose Poems
   at the County Fair
   Existentialism, Pancake House Is Made of Pancakes
   Gerry LaFemina

134 – No Tongue in Cheek: The True Frame of the Prose Poem
   As We Get Closer to the Apricot, The Spine
   Ray Gonzalez

ON METAPHOR: PROSE POEM AS
MORE THAN PROSE POEM

140 – Moving Violations: The Prose Poem as Fast Car
   The Realm of the Wide, Ice
   Maureen Seaton

146 – Whatchamacallit & Me
     I Shall Be Released, Parable of the Astral Wheel
     John Bradley

153 – My Nude Empress
     About the Dead, Crossing
     Nin Andrews

157 – It's Not in Cleveland, but I'm Getting Closer
     Lisboa, 1755, Five Dollars
     Tung-Hui Hu

ON EXPERIMENT: ARRIVING AT THE FUTURE

160 – "Close to You": The Prose Poem: Some Observations
     from The Little Book of Female Mystics, Wish You Were Here
     Mary Ann Samyn

166 – Form and Function: Language in a Double World
     Heavenly Bodies, Subtraction
     Maxine Chernoff

172 – Thoughts on Prose Blocks as Dance and Resistance
     Primer, The Belltown Angel
     Carol Guess

175 – Both Rivers
     After They Plundered the Language, Taking the Psychological Test
     David Shumate

Further Reading 179
Credits 185
Acknowledgments 188
About the Editors 191
A Note About the Type 192

FIELD NOTES
A Preface

In his book *Looking at the Overlooked*, art historian Norman Bryson discusses the distinction between *megalography* and *rhopography*. Megalography, he says, "is the depiction of those things in the world which are great—the legends of the gods, the battles of the heroes, the crises of history." Rhopography, on the other hand—"from *rhopos*, trivial objects, small wares, trifles"—"is the depiction of those things which lack importance, the unassuming material base of life that 'importance' constantly overlooks."

Bryson is talking about still life painting in his book, and we're exploring the writing of prose poetry in this one, but the terms can be applied across the genres to highlight our intentions with the publication of this, our second *Field Guide*.

Our mission at Rose Metal Press is to call attention to literary work in hard-to-categorize and frequently overlooked genres: short short stories, as opposed to, say, novels; novels-in-prose poems or book-length poems instead of traditional collections of poetry. Many writers are writing innovative work in these genres, and yet there are limited opportunities to publish full-length manuscripts, critical studies, and discussions of the form, though that's beginning to change. In particular the topics of our two companion *Field Guides*, flash fiction and now prose poetry, are growing in popularity and opportunity. Both forms gather part of their appeal not from being "mega"—enormous, heroic, grand—but rather from being "rhopo"—small, personal, intimate. Flash stories and prose poems frequently pay heed to subject matter that larger forms might consider too minor to trifle with, or might overlook completely.

Gary L. McDowell and F. Daniel Rzicznek, the editors of this collection, approached us at our table at the massive AWP Book Fair in New York City in January 2008. Under the fluorescent lights, they pitched us their idea for a book that would, as they put it, give readers "a firsthand opportunity to get inside the minds of contemporary poets and see how the prose poem has influenced their lives as artists." They made clear that while they both enjoyed and respected the power of the critical essay, they found the lack of personal essays about prose poetry to be a gap that they wanted to fill.

Intrigued, we told them to put together a proposal and send it our way. In the meantime, we talked to each other about how serendipitous their timing might turn out to be. In November 2007, Tara L. Masih had proposed to us the book that became *The Rose Metal Press Field Guide to Writing Flash Fiction*. Depending on what they came up with, Dan and Gary's book stood to be a perfect complement.

When the proposal showed up in our inbox in March, we were not disappointed. In it, Dan and Gary explained the rationale behind their smaller, more personal approach to the form. "One disadvantage of the critical essay is the possibility of a disconnect between the text and the audience," they wrote. "This is the exact reason we have asked our poets to speak about the impact of the prose poem on their personal lives and aesthetics. We have used the personal essay as a launching pad to get at the critical aspects of the prose poem through personal anecdotes and histories." In asking the authors included herein to approach their essays this way, Gary and Dan hoped to allow the reader—be it a teacher, a student, a writer, or simply a person who likes poetry—"to connect with the author's views and opinions without closing the door on the reader's reactions."

In other words, the editors were not proposing to create some kind of definitive be-all-end-all pronouncement on the genre's shape and prominence, but rather to add more voices to an ongoing conversation about what the prose poem can be and do and say. This approach synched up perfectly with our desire as a press to continue to focus on smaller, stranger forms that gain their importance not by being colossal or well established and canonical, but rather by rising out of a place of relative marginalization and youth to challenge tradition.

Prose poetry, to Gary and Dan and to us, is not just poetry without line breaks. It can and does borrow from forms outside the world of poetry: The editors offered such examples as "questionnaires, conversations, dream narratives, and art installations like the boxes of Joseph Cornell." Blocks, patches, scraps, chunks, fragments. Prose poems are little boxes that can contain big things. Or small things that mean big things. Or small things that mean small things. As you'll see in this book, both in the essays and the prose poems that follow them, prose poetry allows a lot of freedom for subject matter, styles, and voices of all kinds.

We are pleased that Dan and Gary have not attempted a sweeping, large-scale definition or justification of the form. Rather they, like us, want to give readers a chance to look out over the field of literature, notice this form, and treat it thoughtfully and personally. Similar books on larger, more established genres—the novel, poetics in general—are too numerous to count, but, although there are (as you'll see in Dan and Gary's introduction) a few excellent anthologies on prose poetry, there are not very many and none that explore the poets' influences, craft, and experiences with the form.

Dan and Gary's **introduction** offers a history of the form, following the genre from its modern genesis in France in the work of Bertrand and Baudelaire, through its adoption by schools of American poetry, including the deep imagists, feminists, and experimentalists, to its current practice and popularity.

Thirty-four personal essays on the prose poem follow, all written by current practitioners and teachers of the form. Each essay ends with two prose poems by the essayist, making this book half reflective critical study and half anthology, but all personal and engaging. These essays and their examples make great teaching tools, both in the classroom and in the offices, studies, and bedrooms of seasoned and novice poets; but the book is also an enjoyable read for anyone interested in the genre and its rebellious spirit.

Like *The Rose Metal Press Field Guide to Writing Flash Fiction*, this *Field Guide* concludes with a **list of further reading** in prose poetry, suggested by the press, editors, and essayists.

Thus, we are thrilled to offer readers a *Field Guide to Prose Poetry* that operates not unlike a field guide to wildlife, plants, or trees in that it surveys and showcases what the field has to offer while encouraging active engagement with that landscape. We hope readers will use this book as they traipse around exploring prose poetry and finding many, many small things they may never have noticed before—unassuming at first, maybe, but then quite important after all.

–Abigail Beckel & Kathleen Rooney
Rose Metal Press
Boston, MA, 2010

REBELLION STILL HAS ITS ATTRACTIONS
A Case for Prose Poetry

"What grows in that place is possessed of a beauty all its own, ramshackle and unexpected," Campbell McGrath writes in his poem "The Prose Poem" of the ragged but welcoming gully between a field of wheat and a field of corn. Like those agricultural margins with their wildflowers, weeds, amphibians, and songbirds, the prose poem represents an intersection between crops of another kind: nonfiction, fiction, and poetry, three of the four major literary genres of the past three centuries. Perhaps the earliest tradition of prose poetry originated in Asia, specifically China, where the poets of the Han Dynasty (206 BCE–220 CE) practiced a lengthy poem in rhymed prose (called *fu*, and usually translated as "rhapsody" in English) that was as descriptive as it was narrative. However, the prose poem as it is typically identified in Western literature today arrived primarily via the early-nineteenth-century French poets Aloysius Bertrand and Charles Baudelaire, and it has steadily gained popularity in contemporary American poetry ever since.

Used as an alternative to lineated verse (both formal and free) among poets of the last 50 years, the prose poem has been used to myriad ends. Deep imagists such as Robert Bly, James Wright, and W.S. Merwin employed prose poetry after their respective breaks with meter and inherited form. Bly's *The Morning Glory* (1969) stands as an early example of the American prose poem taking up and expanding upon the qualities of its European grandparents. French poet Francis Ponge's groundbreaking 1942 collection of 32 prose poems, entitled *Le Parti pris des choses* or *The Voice of Things*, in particular comes to mind as an influence, since Bly, too, is obsessed in his poems with the object and how observation serves as a gateway into lyric perception. Wright, in *To a Blossoming Pear*

Tree (1977), used prose blocks to write about memory and travel. Wright rejected the term "prose poem" in favor of "prose piece," an interesting distinction considering that he published his prose blocks intermixed with free verse in this and other collections. Merwin's *The Miner's Pale Children* (1970) and *Houses and Travelers* (1977) (now combined in *The Book of Fables* (2007)) both offer short bursts of narrative studded with rich imagery and moments of lyric intensity. Like Ponge, who viewed the prose poem as "a description-definition-literary artwork," the deep imagists used the form to write without the line but with no less rigorous of an imaginative thrust.

Feminist poets have also embraced the prose poem, at least in part because of this very mutability and expansiveness. Lyn Hejinian's *My Life* (1987), for instance, consists of a series of autobiographic (autographic, one might say, since the life being described isn't singular or that of the author, but rather of a concocted, many-faceted self) prose poem narratives. The pieces are poetic, personal, and dialogic; Hejinian narrates an experience of tension between girlhood and womanhood, between naïveté and self-referentiality. The prose blocks that make up *My Life* read like mini-stories told in fabulist detail but with postmodern feminist leanings; they lull the reader with their music and entangle them with their moments of poetic clarity and mystery.

Many experimentalists—among them Paul Violi, Alice Notley, and Leslie Scalapino—have also adopted the prose poem. Two book-length poems, C.D. Wright's *Deepstep Come Shining* (1998) and Rosmarie Waldrop's *The Reproduction of Profiles* (1987), provide particularly outstanding examples of how experimentalist conventions and concepts can be applied to the prose poem. Stemming from the modern prose poetics of Gertrude Stein, Wright and Waldrop write prose poems like a painter paints a cubist portrait: Words and images garner meaning through association and sound rather than through dictionary denotation. Written in mixed prose and verse, *Deepstep Come Shining* takes as its subject a journey through the Carolinas in search of outsider artists. In it Wright is fixated, like Stein in *Tender Buttons*, on the image as seen through a perspective that is not the writer's own—in Wright's case, this perspective is a camera lens. The prose poem form allows Wright to use an almost

Joycean stream-of-consciousness to narrate her adventures. Similarly, Waldrop depends on the sonic qualities of language to communicate meaning. Simultaneously, she creates negative space for philosophical digressions. Waldrop uses the sentence as an argumentative weapon; she steps in and out of sentence-level rhythms and cycles through images to create a whirlwind block of prose that, while experimentalist in nature, depends heavily on the prose poem form.

These movements, along with the New York School poets, L=A=N=G=U=A=G=E poets, and many other schools of poetry, have flourished since the late 1950s when formalism became the exception in an increasingly free verse-dominated culture of poetry. As they grew and developed, each movement adopted the prose poem as a form of inquiry, and the prose poem now holds its own specialized but increasingly visible niche in contemporary letters.

How we, as editors, and you, as readers, poets, writers, and teachers, first encountered the prose poem is, of course, widely varied, but sharing one such story might be helpful in illustrating the growing respect for the form in contemporary literature. Gary's initial encounter with the prose poem exemplifies the broad range and reach of the form. As a first-semester graduate student he was studying Wallace Stevens and was asked to "define and appropriate the imagery in Stevens' 'The Snowman.'" Gary had no idea how to tackle the assignment and so turned to his teacher, Larissa Szporluk, for some guidance. She recommended Gary read a poet who could be considered the complete opposite of Stevens for a while in order to shuffle his brain so as to gain access once again to "The Snowman." Stevens' reality is a product of the imagination as it shapes the world; reality, in a Stevens poem, in other words, is not a rigid set of circumstances but rather an activity in which the reader participates. Stevens' poems engage, passionately, as corollaries to organized intelligence and the reader absorbs, in the unconscious, currents of the imagination as they create. To counteract the "supreme fiction" of Stevens, Szporluk suggested Gary read some Russell Edson, whose prose poems, in scenes of alternate realities occupied by modern everymen and everywomen, enact the lines we self-draw between the sober and inebriated experiences of domestic environments. Unlike Stevens' reality, which is shaped and perceived in the imagination, Edson's reality, his prose poems of figurative and literal domesticity, is unapologetically bizarre and uncanny but never separated from the real. Living in Edson's world for even a moment was exhilarating for Gary, and from there an obsession was born.

Richard Howard writes that "verse reverses—the reader turns at the end of the line—while prose proceeds." If prose proceeds, then what is a reader to do when presented with prose that, in its sentence structure and music, turns? The prose poem's form isn't a negative space, rather it's a positive one, a space populated with the elements of poetry—imagery, music, lyricism, metaphor, simile, alliteration, assonance, and so on—and dependent, though not wholly, on them. The sentence acts the part of the line, and there are fewer traditional rules and governances, but otherwise, the prose poem is, like its lineated cousins, simply a form of poetry.

One of the main arguments one may posit against the "tradition" of the prose poem is its relatively short history. Yet we, as editors, think this comparatively brief lifespan is an important part of defining, defending, and explicating the form. What is recognizable as the prose poem today originated in France in 1842 with the publication of Aloysius Bertrand's *Gaspard de la Nuit*, a collection that borrows the elements of character and scenario from fiction, but eschews plot in favor of descriptions and comparisons that embody the richness and directness of poetry. Traces of the contemporary tradition can be found in Bertrand's sentence fragments and imagistic leaps, as in this passage from Gian Lombardo's 2000 translation: "And, flapping their wings, storks circle the town clock, stretch their necks straight into the wind and catch raindrops in their beaks." When Bertrand describes a set of money scales "creeping out like a spider that doubled its long legs so it could shelter in a tulip tinted with a thousand different hues," the finely wrought and imagistically explosive sentences (not lines!) of contemporary prose poems by Killarney Clary, Campbell McGrath, Tony Tost, and a wide array of others, come to mind.

When Charles Baudelaire, a contemporary (and perhaps rival) of Bertrand's, encountered *Gaspard de la nuit*, he took the prose form and turned it to his own devices. Baudelaire's *Petits Poèmes en prose*, a collection of 51 prose poems also known as *Le Spleen de Paris* or *Paris Spleen*, appeared in 1862 and has become a major influence on the contemporary prose poem. In Louise Varése's 1947 translation of the poem "The Double Room," Baudelaire writes of "a room that is like a dream [...] Here the soul takes a bath of indolence, scented with all the aromatic perfumes of desire and regret. There is about it something crepuscular, bluish shot with rose; a voluptuous dream in an eclipse." *Paris Spleen* has become known not only for its mixture of concrete, nearly biographical subjects and the abstract and sometimes surreal treatments they are given, but also for Baudelaire's impish attitude toward the Paris of his day. In "The Bad Glazier," also from Varése's translation, Baudelaire throws a flowerpot from a sixth-story window at a glazier below, shattering the man's panes of glass. Baudelaire's conclusion? "Such erratic pranks are not without danger and one often has to pay dearly for them. But what is an eternity of damnation compared to an infinity of pleasure in a single second?" Bertrand and Baudelaire used prose to break the hold of the Alexandrine form in French poetry, and while the break with form is well-established in current American poetry, rebellion still has its attractions.

Acceptance for the prose poem, however, has never come easily. Unusual though it was, the form wasn't disapproved of by critics and readers of poetry in Baudelaire's time, but it was seen, a bit later, by such luminaries as T.S. Eliot as an oxymoronic attempt to "revive the stylistic preciousness and technical 'charlatanism'" of the British Decadents, prose poets like Ernest Dowson and William Sharp. Sharp, the author of *Vistas*, a collection of what he calls "prose imaginings," does the work of the Decadents: The pieces value artifice over nature, turn their eye on the relationships between decay and desire, tormented love and shameful memories of passion and fading beauty. The prose form suited Sharp's idea that the rise of the Decadents in the late nineteenth century would differentiate them "from any predecessor in the new complexity, the new subtlety, in apprehension, in formative conception, in imaginative rendering." But even Eliot praised the prose poems of Baudelaire and the "pure prose" of Rimbaud's *Illuminations*; it wasn't the form that presented the problem for Eliot but rather the authorial intention, the *naming* of the form itself.

Charles Simic once wrote, "The prose poem has the unusual distinction of being regarded with suspicion not only by the usual haters of poetry, but also by many poets themselves." The story of the voting for the 1978 Pulitzer Prize in Poetry has been told many times, but it bears repeating here to illustrate said suspicion. Two members of the three-member committee voted to award that year's prize to Mark Strand for his book of short prose musing on death, entitled *The Monument*. The third committee member, Louis Simpson, opposed the selection and ultimately kept Strand from receiving the prize. Simpson objected to Strand's collection on the grounds that it was composed of prose pieces, not lineated ones. Simpson argued that the Pulitzer Prize in Poetry was to honor excellence in verse writing, and after taking his argument to the higher-ups, the committee's selection of Strand was overturned.

It seems that the fact that Strand's *The Monument* was hard to classify exacerbated Simpson's refusal to see the book as a work of poetry. This incident stands as an example of the distrust that some of the gate-keepers of the contemporary American poetry community have of the prose poem as a form. Of course, when Simic's *The World Doesn't End*, a book of mostly prose poems, won the Pulitzer Prize 12 years later in 1990, Simpson's stance seemed even more antiquated than it did at the time. The prose in Simic's book, while poetic, lacked the prettiness that often accompanies verse in favor of surreal narrative retellings of Simic's war-torn childhood in Belgrade during World War II. This push toward a poetic prose that, as Baudelaire wrote, was "flexible yet rugged enough to identify with the lyrical impulses of the soul, the ebbs and flows of reverie, and pangs of conscience" helped identify the prose poem with its forebears in both genres, prose and verse. The poetic prose identified by Baudelaire summarized a whole new branch of writings that, while not in verse and not intended as prose fictions, had as their author's unmistakable intent a poetic objective. The current poetry community's acceptance of the prose poem as a form is evidenced by the many journals, presses, and anthologies devoted singularly or partially to the form.

Many excellent anthologies of the prose poem in English have appeared in the last 30 years and each of them has argued successfully, through a presentation of diverse voices, that the prose poem is a thriving form. The creation of such anthologies began with the 1977 publication of *The Prose Poem: An International Anthology*, edited by Michael Benedikt (long out of print and extremely difficult to find), and then progressed to, among others, *Models of the Universe* (edited by Stuart Friebert and David Young, 1995), *The Party Train* (edited by Robert Alexander, Mark Vinz, and C.W. Truesdale, 1996), *The Great American Prose Poem: From Poe to the Present* (edited by David Lehman, 2003), *No Boundaries* (edited by Ray Gonzalez, 2003), and *PP/FF: An Anthology* (edited by Peter Conners, 2006). Several journals have focused on the prose poem (and sometimes its flash fiction cousin), beginning with Peter Johnson's now-defunct *The Prose Poem: An International Journal* (1992–2000), and continuing today, including, among others, *Sentence: A Journal of Prose Poetics* (2003–present), *Cue* (2004–present), *Double Room* (2002–present), and *Quick Fiction* (2001–present). Presses partial to prose poetry and other literary hybrids have also emerged, including, among others, Quale Press (1997–present), White Pine Press (1973–present), Tarpaulin Sky Press (2006–present) and Rose Metal Press (2006–present). There have also been a few important critical texts on the prose poem, among them Michel Delville's book, *The American Prose Poem* (1998) and "A Brief Stop on the Trail of the Prose Poem" by Carl Phillips in his book of essays *Coin of the Realm* (2004).

Even with the proliferation of presses, journals, and anthologies celebrating the prose poem, something was missing in the literature of the prose poem: a collection of voices disseminating influences, personal histories, motivations, and theoretical approaches to the prose poem form. No one had yet put together the narrative arc of the prose poem's importance in contemporary American letters.

In the spring of 2006, in the mailroom of East Hall at Bowling Green State University in Ohio, the idea for this book took its first awkward and, initially, fruitless steps. In one corner of the mailroom—narrow and lined on one wall with a floor-to-ceiling shelf perforated with dozens of mailboxes—near the letters R-Z was F. Daniel Rzicznek: MFA Bowling Green State University, 2005. In the other, toward the middle in the M-P section was Gary L. McDowell: MFA Bowling Green State University, 2007. Two years apart.

That was us. We never took an organized workshop together. We never sat in the same classroom together. We never had the pleasure of sitting around a table with eight other MFA students to dissect our poems together. However, through a mutual mentor, Amy Newman, we were introduced as poets of similar temperament. Amy was the Visiting Poet during Dan's final semester at Bowling Green and had been Gary's undergraduate mentor at Northern Illinois University. During one particularly productive and furious round of emailing on a warm, windy April day in 2005, Amy convinced Gary to accept an offer to attend BGSU's MFA program for, among many other reasons, the opportunity to meet and study, outside the classroom, with Dan. The first year of our friendship went according to plan, as Amy had predicted it would: We drank beers, traded poems, recommended books to each other, and shared in the festivities common to all writing communities—readings, book launches, panels, and so on. And then, it happened.

During the spring semester of 2006, Gary took a workshop at BGSU and decided that instead of writing poems of differing forms and voices, he would work on a series of semi-autobiographical prose poems that he'd been contemplating for some time. As he did so, the form became a passion. Gary delved deeply into the prose poem; he read them, wrote them, and confided in his new friend Dan and asked him for advice. Dan had also been writing in the prose form, and had been compiling and publishing his own prose poems. Dan had also been weighing the idea of assembling an anthology to help introduce the prose poem to those unfamiliar with it. As they both moved deeper into the form, Dan decided that having a partner in the endeavor would enhance the project.

So, back to the mailroom on that spring day in 2006. It was closing time, 5:00 p.m., and the mailroom was being locked for the night. Gary was walking down the hall to the staircase when Dan emerged, a straggler, one of the last people left in the building. They had been exchanging emails earlier in the day regarding the prose poem and a certain Dr. X's issues with the form—Dr. X didn't agree that it was a form at all, argued that perhaps it was better left alone, disregarded altogether. So Dan pitched Gary the idea, saying, "Hey, let's put together a book of essays about the prose poem. Let's gather some previously published critical and personal prose on the prose poem, enough to fill a book, and see what happens." "Okay," said Gary.

But after a few in-depth searches—scouring books, journals, the MLA database, you name it—our original goal of collecting enough unique material became unrealistic. Our research made it clear that we were never going to find enough previously written essays on the prose poem to make a book. Everything we did find dealt either with the form's history or its critical reception, neither of which seemed of immediate use to us as poets hoping to enlighten ourselves and others about the form and its possibilities. The history of the form was important, but we wanted to hear personal stories and individual revelations from working poets about how they found the prose poem, about how they began practicing it themselves, and about the idiosyncratic motivations that led to their discoveries.

We went back to thinking about *why* we wanted to do this project to figure out *what* we could do next. We wanted to provide readers new to the prose poem with an acceptable entry to it, one that would be both fun to read and informative. We also wanted to provide the seasoned prose poetry reader and practitioner with a set of representative perspectives and voices meant to catalog and showcase the depth of experience and expertise exhibited by contemporary poets working in the form. Both of us came of age in a literary landscape where prose poems were very common and even emphasized. As readers we encountered the prose poem in the work of many contemporary poets, both famous and unknown, and we admired poets such as David Shumate, Arthur Rimbaud, Russell Edson, Mary Koncel, James Wright, Gertrude Stein, Robert Hass, and Harryette Mullen. As students we were given the prose poem right alongside inherited forms like the sonnet, the sestina, and the villanelle. However, it was unclear why certain poets wrote some prose poems, others wrote almost exclusively prose poems, and still others wrote them not at all. What was clear was the form's invitation to experiment and explore without the strategies of enjambment. We decided there was only one way to find answers to these questions: ask those who knew best, the practitioners of the prose poem.

We decided to start from scratch, pool our resources, and get good poets to write good essays for us. We turned first to our former teachers, the teachers who had introduced us to the prose poem: Amy Newman, Gerry LaFemina, Joe Bonomo, John Bradley, Robert Miltner, William Olsen, and Nancy Eimers. Next, we brainstormed a list of other potential contributors who would help bolster our already growing list of dream-team prose poets, and began searching their email addresses out via dozens of university websites. We then sent emails asking for personal essays and poems. Through the kindness of strangers, 20 percent responded that they would at least try something. We sensed momentum and as the essays came in we were happy to see a wide range of experiences regarding the prose poem, some of which emerged from formative classroom moments, but many of which suggested the realms of childhood and pop culture as creative motivators. We hoped that the personal nature of the essays, something we specifically requested of our potential contributors, would make the prose poem something more intimate than a coldly defined poetic form—that these pieces would be less definition, more invitation. The personal approach of the essayists would, we hoped, give the prose poem a personal history, a personal mythology that we felt our future readers would find appealing in the same way one finds personal recollections of trauma and, similarly, of joy more appealing than a dry, academic reportage of the same events. We simply wanted our readers to care.

In reading over our contributors' essays, we began to notice a pattern: Our contributors felt called to question the prose poem's inviolability and ponder why one thing sounds better in prose than in lines. What impulse leads to the perception of an intertwining of form and content? Our essayists have offered a bevy of both delightful and challenging answers. Alongside the essays, we decided to feature two prose poems by each poet. The prose poems we received were of every shape and shade, and resulted in a lot of hard choices on our part. To best capture the diversity of the prose poem, we decided to simply let the essays and poems speak to each other as fluidly as possible, hence the wide range of aesthetics represented. A quick flip through the table of contents and you see poets who have published books exclusively of prose poems (David Shumate, Joe Bonomo, and Carol Guess, for example), poets who have published collections that feature both lineated verse and prose poems (Nancy Eimers, William Olsen, and David Keplinger, for example), and poets who, while they haven't published extensively in the prose poem form yet, are participating in the form in exciting ways.

Julia Johnson writes, in her introduction to *The Mississippi Review*'s Prose Poem Issue (Volume 34, No. 3):

> I loved anything written in the [prose poem] form because the form encapsulated everything I loved about reading literature; prose poems told stories in the most succinct way, but more than that, they were surprising and strange, unexpected, and with each new sentence took me deeper into a place where things needn't be explained.

We agree with Johnson; the prose poem includes the best of both verse and prose: surprise both linguistic and narrative in nature. Johnson further distinguishes her love of the prose poem when she writes, "At the prose poem's end, it seemed over and satisfyingly complete, finished in a way that many short stories and poems are not, wrapped up tightly as if tied with a string."

Johnson aligns the prose poem with its cousins, siblings, parents, and other relatives of lineated persuasion when she writes that:

> [T]he prose poem is a form that requires the same attention as does the lyric in the study of its prosody. In fact, prose poems have it all. They have imagery, pronounced rhythm, sonorous effects, all in density of expression and execution. The prose poem can even contain inner rhyme and meter. The prose poem's length is generally half a page to three or four pages, which just so happens to be the average length of a lyric poem. If it's longer than that, tension is weakened and it becomes more poetic prose than prose poetry.

Exactly! The definition of the prose poem differs little from the definition of any other form of poetry. The question then arises: Why write a poem in prose if it contains the same elements and tropes as a lineated poem? First of all, the one major difference between a prose poem and a lineated poem is the prose poem's reliance solely on the sentence as its rhetorical rhythm, as its gait. The lineated poem certainly relies on the rhythm of the sentence as Charles Wright, Richard Hugo, Hayden Carruth, and many others have proven over the years, but they also rely on the line break as a unit of syncopation and rhythm. The absence of line breaks gives the prose poem its rather obvious name. But why prose poems? Why not just really long lines? We tend to agree with Johnson in that we see "prose poems as poems that rely more on a kind of prose energy than a lyric energy, no matter what the lines are doing, whether carried over, justified, or broken in some arbitrary or a natural kind of way."

Our contributors pose and answer further questions regarding the prose poem, and whether you're a practicing prose poet or not, their questions will inspire and provoke you to create your own answers. If you're reading this book having never written a prose poem (or a poem at all, for that matter) we hope the inspiration and motivation we feel when reading these essays transfers to you and helps you along your way. As a field guide, taken quite literally, our book provides insight for the writer to make use of as he or she continues to search out, read, and write prose poems. We urge you to keep it in your backpack, on your desk, next to your favorite dictionary, or at your bedside, all locales that the prose poem has been known to frequent. Whether it's your first time encountering this thing that's come to be called the prose poem, or another guidepost along your long journey, our book is here to reveal a small window on the vast and potentially limitless universe of prose poetry.

Even after receiving brilliant and beautiful essays and poems from our potential contributors, we realized that the distribution and appreciation of the prose poem have their dangers. At a recent poetry reading in Bowling Green, Alan Michael Parker publicly bemoaned the prose poem as encouraging both sloppiness of craft and lackluster imitation of its European forebearers. While we agree that, like any movement or sub-genre of art form, the prose poem is not without prose poetasters, we feel the very term "the prose poem" has come to define a small, justified block of writing wherein "weird shit happens." Sometimes, a block of writing wherein weird shit happens just isn't enough of a happening for the naysayer, and that's understandable, but it's the prose poem's adaptability that helps it thrive. While these "weird shit" poems are being written, and some of them are mighty good, so too are many prose poems being written that defy this definition. Prose poetry is not merely poetry minus line breaks. It borrows from forms outside the world of poetry, such as questionnaires, conversations, dream narratives, and art installations like the boxes of Joseph Cornell, which Charles Simic wrote about in his book, *Dimestore Alchemy*.

In setting out to select essays and poems from contemporary poets of differing aesthetics and backgrounds, we've constructed a book that anchors in terra firma while aiming at unknown horizons. We've come this far: Poets are writing prose poems (*lots* of prose poems) and have been for years. Ask each poet and they'll give you a different influential example of how they first encountered the form. The prose poem has existed fruitfully (though not without disparagers) for decades now, but this book brings us to the brink of a new genre, one forged of two distinct parents: prose and poetry. The term has been employed before but we feel it is the best way to label these literary misfits. "The prose poem," while still useful and pertinent, relies too much on the singular. Today, poets are writing long poems in prose, whole linked sequences in prose, books of poetry in prose. "The prose poem" implies one distinct work, while "prose poetry" suggests a wider scope and a new way of thinking about what poetry can do. But the question remains, what exactly is a prose poem? What is prose poetry? There is no one correct answer. There are no two correct answers. In fact, there might not even be an accurate enough question with which to wrangle. The best we can do is call it something instead of calling it something else.

In these pages you'll find poets such as Denise Duhamel and Christopher Kennedy, among others, wrestling with their discovery of the prose poem form. Duhamel, as an undergraduate student, discovers the prose poem in a fiction writing class when the professor assigns Jayne Anne Phillips' *Sweethearts*. Kennedy remembers listening to Gene Pitney's story-songs as a child—his first exposure to the narrative music he would later cultivate in his prose poems. You'll also find essays on influence. Alexander Long and Kathleen McGookey, to name just two, detail their early prose poetry influences, which, coincidentally enough, overlap in time and place: the MFA program at Western Michigan University. Other poets that examine their influences include Michael Robins, Jeffrey Skinner, and Brigitte Byrd.

Defining the prose poem remains a challenge, but that doesn't mean that our contributors backed down from it. We've included some intuitive and adventurous essays that gather unique definitions of the prose poem from poets such as David Keplinger, Beckian Fritz Goldberg, Arielle Greenberg, and more. In Keplinger's essay, America's pastime is used as a window into understanding the prose poem. Alongside essays defining the prose poem, our contributors explore the ideas, theories, and concepts related to the form as well. William Olsen, Amy Newman, and Maurice Kilwein Guevara, for example, all contemplate the connections between the theories and the results of their personal histories with the prose poem. And what would this field guide be without some thoughts on craft? As writers and readers, you've undoubtedly wondered *how* the prose poet arrives at the prose poem form and then accomplishes their finished poem. In essays that range from direct advice to personal stories of revelation in the midst of confusion, poets such as Nancy Eimers, Gary Young, and Ray Gonzalez diffuse some wily information on craft.

We round out the book with a look at some of the underlying motivations and techniques our contributors have used in their writing of prose poems. From fast cars and orgasms to the whatchamacallit and Cleveland, Maureen Seaton, Nin Andrews, John Bradley, and Tung-Hui Hu, respectively, deal with the prose poem metaphorically. Finally, David Shumate and Carol Guess, among others, write about the future of the prose poem, write about the prose poem arriving at the future daily and with repeated enthusiasm. Shumate, for example, is drawn to the prose poem for its homeliness, its inelegance, and in truth, he writes an essay that is the exact opposite of each of those terms. All in all, the essays presented here illustrate the enormity and influence of the prose poem. And after each poet's essay, we've collected two representative prose poems as well that will give you the chance to get to see the poet in action while you digest their personal history with the prose poem form.

In his preface to *Gaspard de la nuit*, Bertrand's speaker asserts, "Art's a coin with two antithetic faces," suggesting that one of these faces is "a philosopher with a white beard who's like a snail winding into its shell" and the other is "a blustering and obscene infantryman who struts about town." Anticipating the criticism that may arise regarding this characterization, the speaker states, "While the author of this book has viewed art under this double personification, he does not want to be too exclusive." Neither do we. Our double characterization—prose poetry—is not meant to exhaust or put to rest the discussion of what exactly it is, or even if it needs to be definitively named or characterized, but rather to give us a name to call it as we then get out of the way and move into a discussion thereof. Thus, as Bertrand was "content to sign his work *Gaspard de la nuit*" and get on with the book, so too are we to sign ours.

–*Gary L. McDowell and F. Daniel Rzicznek*
Editors

The Rose Metal Press Field Guide to
PROSE POETRY

Bob Hicok

PROSE POEM ESSAY
ON THE PROSE POEM

Once upon a time there was a little bit of plot and a lotta bit of letting go
of plot. There was putting some pretty in, some sweet tweet, and 'idn't it
swell too when there's fetching kvetching and the weird's plopped in a
box to play with trees and wires and bang the conundrums, though most
of all I adore how marginal the margin becomes: it just falls plumb, Bob,
down the right side, taking out the lineated huffnpuff of breath, leaving
the plainly more said. I've noticed how the long lines run like hair down
the back of poetry or as roads to the anywheres I'd like to go. For instance:
there was this guy I knew in this room of needing someone to look out the
window and feel how the field of a prose poem grows, how like an acre
it spreads across the page with the sense that we need more land to let
language have its say. There are poppies in the field, orange as if all the
world wants to grow up to be California, there's a child buttering an ax,
a cow chewing back and forth, eating the text of grass. The prose poem's
the Texas of poetry, you got miles of miles and miles, then suddenly it's
New Mexico and over, this whooping and hollering, this rodeoing of pros-
ing. Certain questions are answered best with a shrug: why write until
the carriage returns? Cause it's a pumpkin and I want pie. It could also
be that as a blockhead I naturally write in blocks. Whatever the why or is
of it, the longer stride of the poem makes me relax, not like anal iambic
or geez, why diva sestina when you can relatively siesta your way to an

Bob Hicok's *This Clumsy Living* (2007) was awarded the Bobbitt Prize from the Library
of Congress. He has received a Guggenheim and two NEA Fellowships. A finalist for
the National Book Critics Circle Award, his poetry has appeared in five editions of *Best
American Poetry* and been awarded four Pushcart Prizes. *Words for Empty and Words for
Full* will be published in 2010.

opener sense of life? Natural. Like to end, add a sense of no more: the curtain, once raised, has burned. And we go running after happily ever after, which exists in the purity of how, when we turn to look at it, it Eurydices away, into the chance to wait again for spring to be sprung on us, who want so much to want so much, more than have, smother, hold.

Christopher Kennedy

RIGHT MARGIN MAN(IFESTO)
This Is How I Mean

It's tempting when writing a personal essay about how I became a prose poet to manufacture a neat little narrative that provides a timeline of events, all leading to some sort of epiphany whereby I'm somehow imbued with knowledge and find my way through the fog into the light-laden terrain of the initiated. The truth is my sense of how I became anything is spotty, much less how I started writing prose poems, but here's one reasonable overview:

I remember listening to my sister's copy of Gene Pitney's *Greatest Hits* when I was about nine or ten. I was fascinated by the story-songs on that album, in particular "The Man Who Shot Liberty Valance" and "Twenty Four Hours from Tulsa." The narrative combined with the music appealed to me, and I memorized the lyrics and imagined the scenarios they depicted. Around the same time, my mother brought home a book, a rare occurrence in my family. A few years earlier, her father had died of a heart attack, and my father, her husband, had been killed in a car accident one day later. My guess is that someone who wanted to offer her some solace in her grief gave her the book.

The book was a memoir, *Red Shoes for Nancy*, about a young girl born with a degenerative disease whose legs are amputated. Her wish is to own a pair of red shoes. I don't remember much more about the book,

Christopher Kennedy is the author of a collection of prose poems and verse, *Encouragement for a Man Falling to His Death*, which received the Isabella Gardner Poetry Award for 2007, and two collections of prose poems, *Trouble with the Machine* (2003) and *Nietzsche's Horse* (2001). A third collection of prose poems, *Ennui Prophet*, is forthcoming from BOA Editions, Ltd. in 2011. He is an associate professor of English at Syracuse University where he directs the MFA Program in Creative Writing.

except that she gets the shoes in the end. What she did with them is any-one's guess, an absurd irony that perplexed and fascinated me. Around this same time, my mother bought a television with a crude remote con-trol. It was a heavy rectangular object that moved from channel to chan-nel slowly and deliberately. There were only three channels then, and I often found myself home alone after school when the only thing on TV was soap operas. Bored and lonely, I became adept at getting from soap to soap almost seamlessly. I created my own narratives, skipping from one melodramatic scene to another, and I noticed that randomly splicing together the stories created some funny moments. It became my after-school pastime for months. How these instances added up to the creation of a prose poet would take more expertise about the devel-opment of the human brain than I possess, but I don't doubt the influ-ence.

What I do know for certain is that writing prose poems gave me an identity as a writer, and for better or worse, genre-blurring has been somewhat of an obsession for me for a long time. It may be that by embracing the prose poem I've banished myself to some isolated island of misfits, but I find the company compelling.

So last night after I finished writing the previous sections of this essay, I dreamt I wrote a letter to J.D. Salinger, asking him to write a novel "just for me." I ended up hand-delivering the letter, and on the other side of it was a contract for him to give a reading at Syracuse University where I teach. Salinger laughed at my brazen attempt to get him to leave his seclusion, but he told me he was touched by the part of my letter where I wrote that I needed him to write another novel "because it was the only way I could learn more about the human condition." After he quoted me that part of my letter, I looked around and saw there were other writers in Salinger's living room. We all left together, and when I woke up, I told my wife about the dream, and as I did it occurred to me that this notion of "the human condition" and getting to it through someone's writing was why I became a reader. Something about the prose poem when it works puts me in touch with that in a way reminiscent of the first time I read *Catcher in the Rye* in sixth grade and felt a kinship with Holden Caulfield. There was a voice I trusted that taught something about what it means

to be human. I knew I could be friends with Holden Caulfield. I aim for
a voice like that one every time I write a prose poem. It's not likely that
I ever succeed, but some day I hope to find out something more about
the human condition. Until Mr. Salinger honors my dream request, it's
all I've got.

POEMS

Encouragement for a Man Falling to His Death

I'm sorry your parachute is made of cream cheese, but think of the
spectators and their stories, and the asphalt's loneliness until you ar-
rive, abruptly and without pretense. You've heard of Jesus; now you
get to be just like Him. Every eye that holds your image belongs to a
person who will know, once and for all time, what it means to be alive.
Those who loved you most will place a wreath at the exact spot where
you became an exact spot. Footage of your fall will serve as effective
warning to all who believe cream cheese to be a healthy substitute for
silk. I hope this isn't too much for you to learn on your return to our
distant planet, where all is well as well as all is not so well, depending
on where you're headed, the east and west of which you probably
never stop to consider, obsessed as you are with the physics of north
and south.

Personality Quiz

Q: How would you describe your ability to work with others?
A: A lost shoe in a forest.
Q: Who is the person you would most like to emulate?
A: A photograph locked in a trunk.
Q: How would you characterize yourself in an emergency situation?
A: A child lost in a maze.
Q: What is your most interesting quality?
A: A half-finished painting in an attic.
Q: Which celebrity would you like to portray you in the story of your
    life?

A: An exterminator, carrying a spider outdoors to safety.

Q: Is there anything about yourself you would change?

A: A broken lock on a door.

Q: Anything else?

A: A missing windowpane.

Q: How would you like to be remembered after your death?

A: The answer to a question no one asks.

Q: What is your favorite television show?

A: A windmill on fire in a young girl's dream.

Q: If you could be another animal, what would you be?

A: A slab of meat on a conveyer belt, receiving a soul.

Q: How would you describe yourself to others?

A: The problem and the solution.

Q: How would others describe you?

A: A shadow hidden in the shade.

Q: How would you describe your state of mind?

A: A curious beachcomber, glimpsing a tidal wave.

Q: Do you have an ideal vacation spot?

A: The early test sites in Nevada.

Q: Is there a person from your past who has made an impression on you?

A: A priest in line for confession.

Q: If you were an inanimate object, what would you be?

A: 30 degrees latitude, dreaming it's the equator.

Q: How would you describe your social life?

A: A monk on his deathbed with a vision of sex.

Q: How would you describe your time management skills?

A: An hourglass lost in the desert.

Q: Who is your hero?

A: A fish that's developed a fear of drowning.

Q: How would you describe your religious beliefs?

A: A dyslexic psychic, predicting the past.

James Harms

"GOODTIME JESUS" AND OTHER SORT-OF PROSE POEMS

I suspect the reason I can't remember my first encounter with the prose poem has a great deal to do with when I came of age as a poet, the fact that my teachers didn't think of the prose poem as exotic or strange or even particularly sexy. Interestingly, I *can* remember the first time I read James Tate's "Goodtime Jesus," a prose poem that appears in his book *Riven Doggeries*, published in 1979 when I was nineteen. Like a lot of undergraduates of my generation, being assigned Tate in a poetry workshop was a rite of passage and a wake-up call, a little like hearing *London Calling* for the first time (which was also released in 1979). Tate was funny and strange and maybe even a little dangerous; the fact that he often wrote prose poems seemed incidental. In all honesty it still does. I often can't discern a specific or verifiable difference between Tate's poems in lines and those in prose (this is especially true recently, when his work seems written for the most part in lined blocks). I don't doubt that Tate has very good reasons for writing some poems in lines, some in prose, but I can't imagine they'd matter much to the reader.

This leads me to a scandalous assertion (not really, but let's make believe something is really at stake here): I'm not sure it matters all that much whether some poems are lined or not. This isn't to say that free verse poetry lacks rhythmical integrity and/or music, that its relation

James Harms has published six books of poetry, most recently *After West* (2008) from Carnegie Mellon University Press. His second collection, *The Joy Addict*, for which he received the PEN/Revson Fellowship, was reprinted in 2009 in Carnegie Mellon's Classic Contemporary Series. A recipient of an NEA Fellowship and three Pushcart Prizes, he is a professor of English at West Virginia University and also directs the low-residency MFA Program in Poetry at New England College.

to the line is random or convenient; for such tired and tedious arguments, one should consult *The New Criterion* for the company policy on the essential slackness of a free verse line. In fact, I'm arguing the opposite. It seems to me that many, *many* prose poems read like lined verse with the breaks removed. This is true of Baudelaire, Rilke, Neruda, Simic, and any number of wonderfully fluent poets who move back and forth from line breaks to margins. Each of these poets has a sensibility that is recognizable from across the room. They have a way of inhabiting language that no amount of density is going to mask. When they banish the line break, the language retains its essential poetry; in other words, the character of the image and the coordination of phrases (the musical interaction of syntactical units) remain in effect regardless of the poem's "look."

To clarify this a bit (at the risk of running the ship right up the cul-de-sac), let's return to Tate. What makes his poetry distinctive has more to do with the way he occupies space and time than it does with prosody. His prose poems enact a postmodern relationship to everyday life (without acceding to the existence of anything remotely or theoretically *postmodern*) in exactly the same way his lined poems do. For poets like Tate, prose seems an opportunity to do something different with the shape and texture of language, with how we as readers encounter phrases, and how our expectations are undermined and exploited by extending the horizontal momentum of the language while suspending the vertical. But that's just Tate. And that's why reading "Goodtime Jesus" in 1979 didn't register as anything more remarkable than reading another cool James Tate poem (which says something about my undergraduate education: Baudelaire who?).

Still, other poets take advantage of the prose poem to radically change their use of language. As Robert Hass has suggested, the tonal qualities of a sentence are very different from those of a line or phrase; and perhaps for the poet, the sentence allows us to remain a bit more outside of or external to the language we're using; we're not constantly being seduced by the complexifying nature of line breaks, the way they create their own meaning, their own elegance and/or ugliness. Hass has said, "I unconsciously started writing prose to avoid the stricter demands of incantation." In other words, there were some things going on in his life that he wanted to avoid in his work; incantation would have led him straight to these things.

And thank goodness he decided to avoid lyric disclosure for a while. After all, most of us *do* remember encountering *Human Wishes*, that godsend of a book that did more for prose poetry than any collection in recent memory. I'm mindful of the many prose poetry aficionados who find *Human Wishes* somewhat blasphemous, since Hass quite assertively rejects a certain model of the prose poem, what he calls "a kind of wacky surrealist work," which was, in fact, the version of the form that had come to dominate American prose poetry in the 70s and 80s (see Russell Edson and his crew, i.e., Michael Benedikt, James Tate, Bill Knott, Charles Simic, and the rest, all of them wonderful in their own ways). Hass is one poet who uses language differently in prose poems, and has discussed at length the distinctions between story and song, why we need them both and how they require very different things from us as poets; he enacts these differences vividly in his poem "My Mother's Nipples" from *Sun Under Wood*, a poem that moves tensely between psychologically fraught passages of prose recollection (the effort to create distance from the painful memories via prose only serves to underscore the need to limit the emotional toll such memories exact; so much for the less exacting demands of prose) and more descriptive and incantatory stanzas that seem interested primarily in transformation and connection (not so much in recording memory as finding a place for it in the world).

But it's not just the sonic and song-like qualities of lyric poetry that are allowed to recede a bit into the background in the prose poems of poets like Hass and James McMichael (and, a generation before, James Wright and Richard Hugo). The character of the image is different; there is far less resonance, less investment in the silence surrounding concrete details. When I read Hass's prose poems I think of the way Tomas Tranströmer made the transition from deep imagery to a more discursive (and powerful) poetic vernacular; how he began, in the early 70s, to experiment with prose poems that, at first, retained their gorgeously strange and transforming metaphorical images but allowed for more room to talk, more of his coy conversational idiom. Then, slowly, the poems stretched out and moved toward naturalism, though they never abandoned those interior spaces that the early work seemed intent on finding with a flashlight: Reading early Tranströmer is like looking at a photo album of someone's dreams; the later work walks us around the dream pointing out the places in the ceiling where a waking consciousness is leaking in.

Like Tranströmer, Hass is not exclusively interested in the story per se (of the body or otherwise), but he's conscious of the way story organizes experience (interior or exterior), how it shapes reality into paving stones that resemble the sequential (and fictional) paths we walk in everyday life. This resemblance allows for all sorts of things to take place in language that seem less crucial to the lyric temperament of compressed and lineated poems, not least of which is the psychological acuity of plain speech finding its way toward articulation and sense. Certainly plain-spoken narrative poems work wonderfully in lines, but here's the rub: Lined narrative poetry often seems to work in opposition to compression, and the danger of flatness is extreme. The prose poem, on the other hand, is ever mindful of compression: It may look like prose but it's trying like hell to be short, to not resemble a story or an essay. I suppose there's an irony here: In attempting to overcome the limitations of line and lyric length, the lined narrative poem often tends to slackness; in risking the relative slackness of expository language, the prose poem tends toward tightness, toward concision.

There's also something in between all this—a prose poem like Killarncy Clary's, or Aleš Debeljak's—a poem that seems impossible to categorize, whose textures and rhythms are utterly specific to that misty region between poetry and prose: I can't imagine these poems in lines, but they evoke a consciousness that is not easily framed by the sentence. Clary's work, for instance, is gorgeously atmospheric and meditative, yet it resists incantation through discursiveness. The poems often sound like ambitious conversations, and they are nearly always spoken to an unidentified other (which also takes the incantatory edge off the language). I've always felt that line breaks would destroy the drifting and circular intelligence of these poems, the way they move through thought and into silence, from rumination to description and back again. For lack of a better term, they feel horizontal in their rhetorical designs, like waves rushing up the beach, slowly flattening out into foam and a thin sheet of water, then receding back to the depths.

It could be possible that my first encounter with Clary's work (also around 1979, though it might have been a year or two later) was my first true taste of prose poetry. If, for many of us, prose poetry is a way of solving the problem of how to write the poem, how to find its best shape and expression, if we are, in fact, just casting around for the right vessel to pour the poem into, then perhaps those early Tate poems weren't all that representative; they might as well have been written in lines. But Clary's work never seemed as though it could exist in any other form. Which is why, when I read prose poetry these days, I find myself returning again and again to my not-so-scandalous notion that so very much of it would work just as well in lines, might in fact be improved by the demands of lineation. Since the modernists, issues of form seem motivated as much by fashion and politics as aesthetics. This has been good for the prose poem, which is certainly not the maligned and misunderstood stepchild of verse that it seemed to be back in 1990, when Louis Simpson complained (a polite word for it) that Charles Simic's Pulitzer Prize-winning collection, *The World Doesn't End*, was not, in fact, poetry. In all honesty, his argument seemed silly even then. I remember thinking at the time, *Sorry, Louis, that ship has sailed.*

But maybe the point should have been: Is Simic really writing prose poetry, or is he simply removing his line breaks? In Simic's case, it's a tough call, and I'm not sure it matters; I certainly don't think it needed to be anything that the Pulitzer committee considered. They're beautiful poems, and I return to them again and again. Like many forms, the prose poem seems to add to our choices, to give us another option when we can't seem to figure out how to make the damn thing work. And we should all probably admit that those choices are often arbitrary, just a way of keeping us engaged and curious. It seems like hokum to believe that there's an inevitability to a particular poem and its particular form. Then again, maybe I really did encounter prose poetry back in 1979 when I read Killarney Clary's *By Me, By Any, Can and Can't Be Done,* which seemed unquestionably correct and true. And which is probably why I'm a skeptical enthusiast of the form to this day. Thankfully, my skepticism doesn't keep me from enjoying it.

❦

POEMS

Union Station, Los Angeles (The Reagan Years)

So often the man scraped to bits by his latest try at walking through daylight trails sheet music from a pocket, as if the song forever dribbling from his mouth has origins in the world. He stands too close to the tracks, though the porter is gentle with him, guides him behind the broad yellow line on the platform by touching softly the one elbow unexposed (the other scabbed and bruised blue, the shirtsleeve frayed and flapping in the easy wind blowing up from the tunnels).

The problem is the way sunlight slips through holes in the evening air, the sound it makes, like a child choking on water. Union Station never closes, though three times a day it's swept two ways: a man on a rider broom motoring through the tunnels, swerving over bottles and paper napkins; the transit cops nudging to life each sleeping pile of rags and plastic sacks, shooing them through the tall tiled archways toward the parking lot, toward the alleys off Oliveras Street, the 6th Street underpass, to Chinatown or City Hall, the fenced yards beneath the Hollywood or Harbor or Santa Monica Freeways.

It hurts to climb from dreams and shave and dress, to work all day and wait for rush hour to end, to meet Tom and Bob and Jeff and Dwayne in Little Tokyo for a drink before dinner, another after. And then to Al's Bar near the tracks: the Blasters on at ten, the Plimsouls at twelve. The night ends late and everyone is tired but trying not to say so, just walking slowly in the early morning emptiness of Los Angeles, wondering if it's time to give it up and go home.

We'd known him in college: he stood in the drip of a rusted drain pipe somewhere east of Al's, took off his shirt and smiled. "Hey, guys," he said. "Long time no see, etcetera."

It's where you find it: public policy and smaller government, the
trickle down effect, a gray face recently excavated, all those years of
thinking it's enough, hard work and straight dealing, all those years
lifted like dust from an artifact, the wind a soft brush across the lips.
And then the rain of rusty water, memory: part agent, part solvent,
breaking down to bone the irretrievable, the stripped and bruised-
through, the shame. "I'm taking a slow shower," he said. "Now please
. . ." he turned around and spoke over one shoulder. We were looking
for my car. I'd parked it somewhere near the station. "Please," he said
again. "Could I have some privacy?"

Harvest News

"Mint was showing promise.
The dry bean harvest progressed with slower
drying due to cooler temperatures. Lemon
and grapefruit picking continued. The olive
harvest had begun."
—from *The Modesto Bee*, Modesto, CA

And down Highway 99 my friend Jose found himself unwilling to wait
any longer. Without money she wouldn't love him. Without money he
couldn't stay. The culvert along the service road brimmed with dust,
an old tennis shoe, two beer cans and a plastic sack, all of it waiting
for the rush of drainage, the winter rains after harvest. He watched
the Sierra move within its cloud shadows, the crows on the highway
picking at a carcass, hopping to the shoulder as cars stormed past
then returning to the dog, who took the blows of tires with a ruffle
of fur in the sudden breeze. When the truck pulled over, Jose swung
up into the bed, rapped the window and settled in beside a man who
slept the whole way to Fresno, never stirring beneath his hat, who
woke in time, in darkness, to help hold apart the barbed wire so Jose
could squirm through. And they harvested till midnight, the moon-
less night a sleeve stitched shut, a cape of crow's feathers, a pail of tar.
The moonless night painted their faces black, sketched them gone
until they left, until they took the baskets back to the truck then up
to Modesto, the Farmers Market, where no one would know or care
whose fields, whose hands, whose pockets.

David Daniel

DISCOVERING THE PROSE POEM IN NORFOLK, VIRGINIA

Without knowing it really, I was raised in the mid-19th century. Everything I thought was beautiful—or certainly poetic—was precious, garreted, romantic, lush, elegant, lit by candle, vaguely British via Nashville, morose, and very pretty. It didn't occur to me for many years that I had nothing in common with any of these characteristics but one—moroseness, from the same Latin root, I imagine, as moron—which I had in spades, and it certainly didn't keep me from writing years of lovely, moronic poems. Sadly, however, I didn't write in a manner that likely would have brought me fame and fortune in certain tidy, if bitter, neighborhoods of the poetry world. I was too lazy, for one thing, and for another, what passed for formal verse struck me (strikes me still) as what my father would have written had he not, instead, fabricated lighted polystyrene nativity scenes for Poloron, Inc. So I was in a quandary: full of feelings, longing for fame, utterly ignorant, and with no idea what to do next. It was time, of course, for graduate school. And while I resisted with mulish force the wisdom of my remarkable and patient teachers, David St. John and Charles Wright, something of it and the European influence in their own work seeped in—Rimbaud, in fact, began to flood in, much like the tropical storms in Boston this summer have rushed into my basement, threatening to bring down the house into one muddy ooze.

But it wasn't until I was out of school, living in Norfolk after sell-

David Daniel is the author of *Seven-Star Bird* (2003), which won the Levis Reading Prize. His second book, *Crash and Other Assorted Love Songs* is forthcoming from Graywolf. Recent poems have appeared in *The American Poetry Review, AGNI, Witness, The Literary Review, Poetry East, Antioch Review*, and *Post Road*. He directs the creative writing program at Fairleigh Dickinson University.

ing used cars in Baltimore, spending more and more time in bars with increasingly dangerous characters, watching relationships explode like Challenger clips, that I finally realized how alien my experience of the world was from my means of expressing it. Honestly, I think it was Norfolk, home of the prose poem, where civilization as we dreamed it might be was transformed into a massive Walmart-By-The-Sea. I took a train from Norfolk to Boston in those days and described it as a rolling climb up the evolutionary ladder, with each swoosh of the doors, passengers were replaced with newer, better models until I arrived in the promised land. It was hilarious, at the time—and smug. But what I came to realize, for better or worse, was that it was just the opposite: Norfolk was America—everything else was nostalgia. I needed a form that could express that.

In Norfolk I was a letter writer, and a pretty good, if desperate, one. I wrote those letters on a Smith Corona electric that I got for graduating college; it was a glorious beast—a mutt, to be sure, and beige—and typing on it was almost exactly like being dragged behind the self-propelled Sears lawn mower I used to mow five acres of Tennessee wasteland as a boy—character-building, my father would have said if he had taken a more charismatic approach to parenting. Anyhow, I never really learned to type but I could move my fingers very quickly, which, when combined with the vagaries and violence of the Smith Corona, created interesting effects that were just too difficult to correct. Somehow those letters captured something (whenever I'd type "soul", for instance, it always came out "sould", which I took greatly to heart) that seemed truer to my experience than the poems I labored over with parchment and a vintage fountain pen. One particularly miserable night in Norfolk, when I couldn't even drink myself out of there, I fired up the Smith Corona, and instead of writing friends, I wrote, without thinking about it, a prose poem. And then another, and for weeks I kept doing it, and I'd never had so much fun in my poemwriting life; it was like breathing pure oxygen—and they were (to me at least) funny, something I'd never thought to be before. They were still morose, of course, but they made me laugh, and they felt free of something I didn't know I'd been bound by.

More and more, prose poems became a part of my writing and reading life until I no longer noticed them as significantly different. In my recent poems, I mix lined and prose sections without much worry. They could probably be all prose, but they're so long that I don't want to add another aspect to the ridiculous debates: "How long can a prose poem be before it's a plain old short story?" Prose poems (or prose sections of poems) are, like the Smith Corona, simply a different instrument with different tonalities upon which to fiddle my tunes. I turn to them as intuitively as I turn to one of my dozen guitars or dozens of other stringed or keyed things that lie around my house. I'm perpetually trying to widen the figurative, if not the literal, margins of whatever I do, and I'll use whatever tools might work. (For my current book, for example, which has a lot of prose in it, I've primarily used a very bold and fast one mm gel pen on a 24lb 100% recycled cotton sheet that can absorb a lot of ink so I can be fast without much mess—or with just the right amount of mess—and the manuscripts are, to me, like canvases.) There is, to my mind, a greater notion of a poem's formal integrity than the pin-headed ones that generally dominate the discussion of "formal" poetry; great poetry—great writing of any kind—is bound by the deep, shockingly complex music of its language, which transcends the simple, overt manifestations of formality which themselves are just nostalgia, a painful longing for an order that has never and will never exist. There is beauty there, to be sure, but it is of a very limited sort when it's not part of a broader landscape that includes also the music of the world itself as it sprawls in front of us. The prose poem in the hands of Russell Edson, Rimbaud, Robert Hass in his brilliant *Praise*, and, conversely, the "poem prose" in the hands of such masters as Juan Rulfo, helped me discover this. Way back, I sent that first batch of prose poems to *Witness*, and, miraculously, they accepted all of them. When the magazine came out, I discovered they were accepted and published as short stories, which, while surprising at first, seemed perfectly fine to me. At the time I was enthralled by Rulfo's *Pedro Paramo*—that 130-sparsely-worded-page novel—which was to me as much a poem as my beloved *Paradise Lost*; that is, whatever I look for in great poetry was there and in much greater abundance than in any living poet I'd read. Is it a poem? A prose poem? Of course not. But once rhyme and meter are abandoned, any absolute distinction between great poetry and great prose is arbitrary—useful and necessary at times, but arbitrary nonetheless. Over the last year, I've been asking—tongue somewhat in cheek—any poets who'd listen to define poetry without rhyme and fixed meter as distinct from prose. Everyone—every single one—laughed, and then said something about "the line" and mentioned this or that essay on "the line." Fair enough, I'd say, but when I pushed and said that, except in rather extreme examples, most of what's indicated by a line is indicated in the language itself with or without its lineage (so to speak), everyone responded with something like this: "Well, we all know poetry and good poetry when we see it, even if it's impossible to define clearly." And I completely agree with that, whether we see it in something called a novel, a short short, a poem, or a prose poem. That response is a kind of riff on Louis Armstrong's well-worn definition of jazz: "If you gotta ask, you'll never know."

And as with jazz for a jazz player or fan, it's not that we know it because of any innate or special wisdom; we know it, rather, because we've spent our lives with the noises of great traditional music or poetry dancing in our heads, the essence of which is alive and recognizable and to be celebrated in whatever form it comes, prose poem or not.

POEMS

Paint

White, he said, *I'm going to paint everything white. Good*, she said, *It's about time, it's time to paint everything white. Yes*, he said. And he pulled out a large brush and painted the words *everything* and *white* on the wall in a very attractive hand, words which happened to be the first two of the novel he'd just begun writing of the same name. She was not amused. *I'm not amused*, she said. *Paint, this place is filthy.* He painted the words *was kept in a separate room* across the wall and onto the window, then *until the snow fell and it was taken outside which is when they met...* and on and on until walls were filled and the floor, the plants, the couch, the lights, the pages of books, the words, the chapters, becoming indistinguishable. She said, *The place looks great, you're a good painter. Thanks*, he said, and he took off his clothes to begin the last chapter on his legs. It was a love story, but also a mystery because it turns out the two lovers had been dead all along. *Dead people can't be characters*, she said, *It's not right*. And she took off her shirt and pants and said, *Paint, it can't end like this*. Of course, it could end any way he wanted, so he kissed her as he painted *yes* over and over until she disappeared.

Hotel

The phone rang. It rang all the time, even when it was answered, and it was answered often enough—*Hello, hello*….She said, *The phone is ringing*, and he said, *I know, it rings all the time*—which is when it rang. But how it rang—through the doors, the windows, down the halls, the stairs, in every room, remained a mystery, a mystery that made them love one another all the more. She said, *I love you all the more because the phone is always ringing. Hello*, he said, *Hello*. She said, *We need an answering machine. Yes*, he said, *What could we say on it? Hello*, she said, *Hello*. Which is what he'd hoped because anything else would have disappointed and he might have even taken the phone off the hook, which wouldn't have mattered since the phone rings anyway, but which would have had symbolic significance. She said, *Do you think the ringing has any symbolic significance? Oh yes*, he said, *No question*. The message someone left on the machine was the sound of a phone ringing, which both found inexplicably exciting.

Andrew Michael Roberts

ENCHILADAS FOR THE STOLEN BOYS
A Personal History of the Prose Poem

One evening last week, I sat across from my brother at Café Frida in Manhattan over astronomically priced enchiladas and margaritas. It was his birthday and he was nearing drunkenness. As usual with my brother, protocol demanded I distract him from potential embarrassing public outbursts by running him through a quick succession of stories about our childhoods spent in the backwoods of western Washington State. Five minutes into my barrage of anecdotes, he stopped me with a gesture, laid down his fork and said, "Do you remember the time we were stolen by that neighbor guy in a mask who stripped us naked, stuffed us into big suitcases, and tickled us with feathers?"

For my brother, alcohol is truth serum.

"I have no memory of that," I said.

"You were three years old."

"That's the year Mom left."

He raised his margarita in a mock toast, said "Happy fucking birthday to me," and sliced into his enchilada.

Two days later I woke up and wrote a poem:

This Shunt in the Eye of the World

And then there was the time the neighbor man in his gas mask stuffed us each in a suitcase and tickled our testicles with a peacock's blind eye. God, his handsome hello. He wanted us buried.

Andrew Michael Roberts' collections are *something has to happen next* (2008 Iowa Prize, 2009 Oregon Book Award Finalist), *Dear Wild Abandon* (2007 PSA National Chapbook Award), and *Give Up* (2006). He lives in the Sunnyside neighborhood of Portland, Oregon.

He tied us together, his laugh a tin cat. It crawled out of itself. In the clouds of his eyes pear blossoms bloomed. Called us both Sugar Bee, and the drones dropped out drowned. I enjoyed their damp thuds on the astroturfed porch. They stung as they crushed underfoot. We killed and cried out. Brother, he fucked and we liked it. Our ears the whining of saws, his cast iron teeth forced inside. Too soon from the woods barking our old names came the dogs we'd forgotten wearing masks of the people we loved.

There are also poems for the mothers—one who named me and disappeared, one who couldn't help, in her rages, breaking household items over her boys and punching holes in the slammed-and-locked chipboard doors of our singlewide mobile home:

The Legacy

My mother, the incredible shrinking woman. Little by little she was disappearing and would one day be gone completely. This sort of thing is difficult to accept, and I never blamed her for being indignant, for boozing it up and taking it out on me, her incredible shrinking boy. 'Look at you, you're nothing!' she'd scream, tipping back the bottle. 'You'll never be anything! Never go anywhere!' But she was wrong. I may have been shrinking, but I wasn't nothing yet. And I was going places. Every morning I checked in the mirror—I was getting farther and farther away.

There are childhood memories of three-legged, elk-chasing dogs, 40-foot papier-mâché slug floats crafted for the annual slug festival parade, farm boys on flatbed trucks shooting arrows at passing cars, drunken drag races, gunfights with .22 rifles. Recluses, rapists, farmers, loggers. My father: the policeman, the bodyguard, the medic, the teacher, who taught me to be my own self in a world that would try to strip it from me.

There's the day years later that Rick May, a Portland State University student, leapt from a three-story skybridge over Broadway and landed on his skull. Standing at a crosswalk, I saw him drop. Trained as an EMT, it was my duty to hold his brains in and breathe for him while he emptied of blood and the ambulance arrived to transport a corpse. That he wanted to die and I was required to try to save him haunts me still.

There are the memories of Iraq my brother screams in his sleep every night. When he stays with me, I must use earplugs to get any rest. Every day for him is a nightmare of gunfire and contrails and the biochemical weaponry poisoning his blood.

These are my influences. The losses, abandonments, violations, the dangerous and unforgettable days of a youth in the woods, five miles from the nearest backwards hick town. The humor and pain of the adults who shared them. These are the forces that converge on my consciousness when I sit down to write. They lay heavily on the psyche that now watches the daily world for its strange, small stories. It is the power of language to transport and connect. It is the daily discovery that like me, everyone has some small thing to say.

The prose poem became the form in which I say it.

I came to real writing informally, on my own. In school, teachers told me what to write and when to do it. I was a good little prisoner, earning straight As. But it was at home, alone with ghosts, that I wrote for real. I would run naked in the woods. Away from anyone. It cleansed me. I would find a place to sit and write. Poems. Letters. Anger in words, love I found in the green veil surrounding me, the creatures who inched close, afraid I was human. Perhaps this is where the future prose poems were cultivated—this space in which I found freedom from confines, these moments of abandon where writing became me. Later it would be the freedom of the prose poem form that captured me. No line breaks to stop me, no strict plot to drive me, just an ear for the sentence and a letting go of expectations. Of course I now write and love lined poems as well, but the prose poem is what I always return to. It's curious to me now to think that perhaps my desire to control my surroundings—I was alone in the woods, in a tree, in a cabin I built away from anyone, where no one could change me—was what brought me to such a freeing form of writing stripped of many of the confines lined poetry or traditional fiction can dictate.

It was Sherman Alexie who first gave me the prose poem. I related to Alexie's work immediately. Like him, I grew up poor amid prejudice and dysfunction. He wrote his life into fiction, into gritty stories and poems that fire warning shots at the heart. One day in 2001, I picked up his first book, *The Business of Fancydancing*, and read my first prose poem:

Independence Day

"It was the worst goddamn thing I ever saw," the Old Man tells me. "I was working out on the Reservation last summer. Fourth of July. The Smoke Shack was selling fireworks, had it all stored in the basement and about three in the morning, it explodes. Turned out some little Skin broke in, you know, and we guess he didn't want to turn on any of the lights, so he flicked his Bic and up it went. Anyway, we're sifting through the ash, before we even knew the kid was there, and I kick something. I look down and it's the kid, just his head. I yell over to one of the Tribal Cops and he goes over, picks the head up and boots it like a damn football, thirty or forty yards. Fucking kids, the Tribal Cop yells, walks back to his car, climbs in, and drives off. I couldn't believe it," the Old Man tells me. "I never thought a head could travel that far."

The power inherent in so much tension created by brevity and mastery of voice shocked and fascinated me. The colloquialism and sarcasm offset the grave seriousness of the subject matter. It was brief and beautiful. It struck with great force in the span of a few inches on the page and made me feel. This power caught and kept me.

At the time, living in Portland, Oregon, I'd been struggling unsuccessfully with writing short stories for two years. So I began to mimic Alexie and scour the bookstores of Portland for other prose poems. First I found *The Very Thing That Happens* by Russell Edson, whose fabulist cubes juxtaposed Alexie's straightforward historicity and allowed me to let go some of my realist tendency. Edson led naturally to James Tate (whose "Goodtime Jesus" is still the poem I enjoy the most), Tate to Charles Simic, Simic to John Ashbery to Baudelaire to Max Jacob. Jacob led me eventually to Jean Follain, perhaps the greatest prose poet with his intelligent grace, his quiet power to illicit awe, his microscopic— yet fully alive—attention to detail, his lust for life that is so obvious in his poems. Follain, in turn, led me to Stuart Friebert and David Young's anthology, *Models of the Universe*, which led me to Vallejo and Rimbaud and…

Eventually I found my poems. Exactly how they are born is a mystery to me. I sit down to write and the sentences come. They do not feel like lines begging enjambment, so they run past the edge of the page. But they are compressed, lyrical, carefully listened to. Then they are painstakingly revised for imagery and attitude. They are read aloud. But mostly the process is something I do not wish to examine too closely. There is a mystery at work that asks to be respected.

What I think I know for sure: The prose poems that come most days are strange brothers. They run naked through the woods. They are insatiable for what they won't allow themselves to have. They are uncomfortable in their own skins. They grow quiet in a crowd and slip to the corner to watch and see who wonders where they've gone. These poems meant well. They always wanted to be popular and courageous. Better looking. Better endowed. They admire the guile of mystics and pole-vaulters. They intended to learn kickboxing. They meant to ride motorcycles. They meant to have their shit figured out by now. There they are, centered and justified, pretending to care less whether or not you read them.

POEMS

Love Crushed Us with Its Big Death Truck

and kept driving, and night clapped shut again behind it. Now the house is holey. The bed. We lie here differently. Quiet like fruits. From above in the dark we look halved and opened up. We are covered in skin and tiny hairs.

I have done terrible things. I would sell my books, turn my houseplants ninety degrees every day. They would be healthy and well-rounded.

Are you still awake? Do you wonder if I wonder?

A fly in a waterglass is a kind of poorly designed boat. I hear the ply of hairy oars and think of standing and flapping. I think until I fall sleep. I fall and sleep the sleep of the drowned.

Signs of Life

This drudgery deep in the suburbs. The constant washing clean of sport wagons and the feeding of flourishing stepfamilies. It is one way to go. I shoot up a flare. With my machete, I'm hacking my way out. Someone beat a trail to me and bring the best medicine doctors. Bring your cameraman and military helicopter. I am an undiscovered species. I am the last of my kind. By day I sleep in the shrubbery. Cars rush past, dogs on walks. At night I get the feeling the moon is following me. Its keen yellowy slit. I act like shadows, dogged. To be seen is to be gradually taken back into the fold. This is no walk in the park. This is bushwhacking. This is burying a horse with your hands. Your kidney cleaning someone else's blood. Moth in a hurricane. I am blocks away now, and freedom looks like the far side of this expressway. That treacherous twilight dodge. The squinty moon slips behind a mushroom cloud, and I bolt from the shoulder. Surely someone back there remembers my name. Someone's maybe missing me to death.

Denise Duhamel

HAPPY (OR HOW IT TOOK ME TWENTY YEARS TO ALMOST "GET" THE PROSE POEM)

In 1983, as an undergraduate at Emerson College in Boston, I took classes in poetry, fiction, and writing for young adults. I don't remember any hard and fast rules regarding poetry and prose—we wrote prose and poetry for young adults, paragraphs in the fiction class (many of which were probably technically for young adults since most of us were still obsessed with our childhoods that were not so long ago) and similar prose blocks for poetry workshops. In one of those classes—and I can't remember which one—my professor Jack Gantos assigned *Sweethearts* by Jayne Anne Phillips. The chapbook, originally published in 1976, was, according to the last page, from an edition of "2,000 copies in its third printing." I treasured *Sweethearts*, which has a wedding portrait of Phillips' parents on the front cover, the first prose poem in the book being an ekphrasis describing that photo. I didn't know then if the writing in *Sweethearts* was prose or poetry—I don't remember even asking the question. I hold the book in my hands now—there is no blurb or description that would clue the reader into the genre of the book. Jayne Anne Phillips has a short bio in the back, but that states only that this is her first collection. Apparently, I paid $3.95 for it.

I'm not even sure if Jayne Anne Phillips would consider the work in *Sweethearts* prose poetry because her first full-length book, 1979's *Black Tickets* (in which work from *Sweethearts* is reprinted), was marketed as fiction. But for the sake of this essay, I am asserting that *Sweethearts*—

Denise Duhamel's most recent poetry titles are *Ka-Ching!* (2009), *Two and Two* (2005), *Mille et un Sentiments* (2005), and *Queen for a Day: Selected and New Poems* (2001). A recipient of a National Endowment for the Arts Fellowship, she is an associate professor at Florida International University in Miami.

a book of prose blocks, none of which is longer than a page—was my introduction to the prose poem. The piece that most impressed me in the book and stayed with me all these years is called "Happy." I include it here in its entirety:

> She knew if she loved him she could make him happy, but she didn't. Or she did, but it sank into itself like a hole and curled up content. Surrounded by the blur of her own movements, the thought of making him happy was very dear to her. She moved it from place to place, a surprise she never opened. She slept alone at night, soul of a naked priest in her sweet body. Small soft hands, a bread of desire rising in his stomach. When she lay down with the man she loved and didn't, the man opened and opened. Inside him an acrobat tumbled over death. And walked thin wires with nothing above or below. She cried, he was so beautiful in his scarlet tights and white face the size of a dime.

I remember writing in my journal about the ambiguous "it" in the second sentence. Was the "it" the love the speaker felt for "him?" Or the happiness? Was "it" the man, a sort of "he" that was not human? Was "it" the "thought of making him happy," the same "it" of sentence four? Could a writer do that? Invert the pronoun with the antecedent? Was the "soul of the naked priest" the man she loved and did not? The transition from the philosophical bent (what is it to love a man and not love a man?) to the breathtaking imagery of the ending moved me and taught me about the power of poetry in a visceral way. The concrete acrobat tumbling over abstract death with his "white face the size of a dime" was a kind of surrealism I could hold onto because it resonated with me on an emotional level.

Around the same time (and perhaps for the same class), Gantos also assigned James Tate's *Hottentot Ossuary*, a small press book published by Cambridge's Temple Bar Bookshop. This book was published in 1974 in an edition of 1,500. The title piece is 14 pages long and re-reading it now it does read to me like prose, but there were more than several prose poems in that collection, my favorite of which is "A Beginning," a comic poem in which two men are trying on "semiformal wear" in a Salvation Army. While Phillips had employed dream imagery, Tate's vignette was another approach—deadpan and detached—that excited me. Also equally important were the more earnest and meditative prose poems of James Wright—especially "Honey," from his book *This Journey*, published in 1982.

I came to poetry via fiction. I'd won an undergraduate scholarship for creative writing (a short story), but when I first came to college, I truly had no idea that anyone was writing contemporary poetry, so Phillips, Wright, and Tate—and poets such as Bill Knott and Thomas Lux, both of whom taught at Emerson—opened my eyes to the possibilities of narrative poems and lyrical fiction. I didn't study the prose poem seriously as a genre unto itself until much later, until after completing my MFA at Sarah Lawrence in 1987. I only started to put it all together in 1992 when I purchased a copy of Peter Johnson's literary magazine *The Prose Poem: An International Journal*. In the first volume he asserts, "Just as black humor straddles the fine line between comedy and tragedy, so the prose poem plants one foot in prose, the other in poetry, both heels resting precariously on banana peels." Shortly thereafter I heard Johnson at a conference say something to the effect that poets sent him work that he didn't believe was as well crafted as their poems in lines. He suggested that some poets, without the line to guide them, had a tendency to get sloppy—and he talked a bit about the history of the prose poem. It was after hearing him speak that I returned to Edson and Simic, Rimbaud and Baudelaire. Shortly thereafter I became aware of and a fan of Johnson's own prose poetry as well as the work of Nin Andrews and Nancy Lagomarsino. I had before then felt comfortable writing prose blocks, but I started to write them with more frequency and urgency.

As a professor at Florida International University, my favorite class was a graduate form and theory seminar called The Prose Poem that I taught in the summer of 2002. To prepare for it, I read *The American Prose Poem* by Michel Delville and *Boxing Inside the Box* by Holly Iglesias. (The latter had not been published yet, but I was able to get a copy in manuscript.) I had the students write neo-surrealist prose poems, "miniature" prose poems, "portrait" prose poems, imagist prose poems, fabulist prose poems, and meditative prose poems. Several students in

ere fiction writers and the inevitable questions arose: What is
ıem? What is a short short? How are they different? I brought
ıdrew's *The Book of Orgasms*, a book of prose poems that is
stamp "fiction" on the back. I sent my students to *Double Room*, the
online literary magazine featuring poetic prose. Contributors are asked
to answer a question relating to genres, one of which is: What is the dif-
ference between a prose poem and a flash fiction?

I read them my answer:

Prose poetry and flash fiction are kissing cousins. They are kissing on
Jerry Springer, knowing they're cousins, and screaming "So what?" as the
audience hisses. They're kissing on *One Life to Live*, unaware one's aunt
is the other's mother. A prose poem suffers from amnesia, and when her
friends tell her about her past, nothing they describe produces in her
even a flicker. In a flash, she thinks: they are wrong—something tells me
I was once a short short. Flash fiction looks into the mirror and sees a
prose poem. A prose poem parts his hair on the left instead of the mid-
dle, and his barber tells him he's flash fiction. A prose poem walks into
a bar, and the bartender says, "What'll you have? The usual paragraph?"
A flash fiction walks into the doctor's office and the doctor says, "How's
that stanza feeling?" There may be a difference between flash fiction and
prose poems, but I believe the researchers still haven't found the genes
that differentiate them.

I asked my students to answer the questions themselves. In answer-
ing the question, some of them inadvertently wrote prose poems.

When Jayne Anne Phillips' *Black Tickets* was published as a Delta/
Seymour paperback, the black and white photograph of her parents
from *Sweethearts* appeared instead as a color painting by Joanne Pen-
dola. I am tempted to close with a metaphor in which prose poetry and
flash fiction are like paints and cameras trying to capture the same sub-
ject. But I will resist the temptation to classify, just as prose poems con-
tinue to resist.

POEMS

Embarazar

The Dairy Association's huge success with the campaign "Got Milk?"
prompted them to expand advertising to Mexico. It was soon brought
to their attention the Spanish translation read, "Are you lactating?"
This worries me because I am in Spain and my period is over a week
late. *Café con leche descafienado con sacarina, por favor.* You're not
supposed to have swordfish when you're pregnant, so I order it. My
body refuses to give me a hint. I feel no premenstrual bloating, no
breast swelling, no backache. I feel no morning sickness, no crav-
ings. I feel my stomach for signs of a heartbeat. I imagine my breasts,
spilling over with *leche. When Parker marketed a ballpoint pen in*
South America, its ads were supposed to have read, "It won't leak in
your pocket and embarrass you." The company thought that the word
"embarazar" (to impregnate) meant to embarrass, so the ad read: "It
won't leak in your pocket and make you pregnant!" I fear my hus-
band's pen has leaked into my pocket. I look at my calendar figuring
out when I can schedule an abortion once we get home. I wonder
if we should drive up to France, where I'm pretty sure I could find
RU486, the French Abortion Pill, which, if it's ever marketed in the
United States, will be called Mifepristone. Or I wonder if we should
keep the baby (who would come in January) and figure out a place
to fit a crib in the apartment. Today we saw a Down syndrome girl
on the bus biting her arm. I'll be forty by the time the baby comes.
Frank Perdue's chicken slogan, "It takes a tough man to make a ten-
der chicken" was translated into Spanish as "It takes an aroused man
to make a chicken affectionate." My husband has been aroused a lot
lately, like Frank. We are on vacation, which makes me affectionate.
I want to buy one of those little pregnancy test kits, but it is Sunday
so all the *Farmacias* are closed. My husband has always been care-
ful about putting a cap on his pen, and I have always been diligent
in making sure he does, but now I remember that one awful time
that we were so in a hurry doing laundry that one of our Papermates
turned a whole batch of whites blue.

Napping on the Afternoon of My 39th Birthday

A man sits between my husband and me at the movies, then puts his hand on my breast and says, "Let's go." I say, "Excuse me, I'm here with my husband..." But my husband hushes me and points to the screen. The man says, "Your wife and I will meet you in the lobby," and without looking up, my husband says, "OK." The man pushes me against the wall—he has some kind of coarse beard and his pubic hair is all prickly. I'm screaming for my husband, but he never comes. I don't do anything to save myself—no karate chop, no biting, no clawing. I want to be saved by my husband, but I'm not.

The bearded man takes me to a rodeo and says, "This is how it's done." The big animals are fucking and the females are screaming— they aren't bulls or cows, but something even fiercer. I say to the man, "You are my nightmare." Then the same man is buying me ice cream and we are friends, maybe even married. My real husband never comes to get me which probably has nothing to do with him, but instead is about my anxiety. It may even be a basic lesson—how I have to save myself. Or a primitive fantasy that I want to be taken, no matter how brutal. Most probably, it's all about fear.

In the hall I meet up with two women who have been scorned, and we storm into the man's apartment. I'm going to help them do what—kill him? We are dressed like Charlie's Angels and the man is the same man who raped me, who then bought me ice cream. He is watching some kind of pornography—women and snakes. We toss the TV on top of him. His feet curl up, a la the Wicked Witch, while the TV smokes and our clothes evaporate. Then we are, all three of us, women with big round butts and tiny waists. We prance around wearing only gossamer wings, the height of desire on a 19th-century sepia postcard.

Brigitte Byrd

I CANNOT ESCAPE THE PROSE POEM

Who among us, on an inspired day, has not fancied the miracle of a poetic, musical prose
without rhythm and without rhyme, fluid yet disjointed enough to adjust itself to the
lyric movements of the soul, the undulations of reverie, the jolts of consciousness?

—Charles Baudelaire

As a poet, I open myself to what Baudelaire calls "the lyric movements of the soul, the undulations of reverie, the jolts of consciousness." My work is the expression of this psychic/intuitive/spiritual/mystical experience, and the prose poem is the form that best fits this expression for me.

I came to realize that the prose poem fits my natural voice after trying to reject it by imposing a temporary formal structure on my work through an experiment with sonnets. After writing my first collection of prose poems, *Fence above the Sea*, I felt the urge to go back to lineated verses. Somehow, I had managed to convince myself that I had to move on to a different form so that I would not limit myself to the prose poem. I then decided on writing crowns of sonnets with a French twist and composed in Alexandrines. Although I enjoyed this experiment and framed my second book *The Dazzling Land* with two crowns of sonnets, I soon realized that my natural voice was under siege and that I needed to face the obvious—that I am at home writing prose poems. It is not easier. It is not harder. It is just me. As the poet William Matthews puts it, "I imagine one is drawn to write prose poems not by sloth, which is better

A native of France where she was trained as a dancer, *Brigitte Byrd* is the author of *Song of a Living Room* (2009), *The Dazzling Land* (2008), and *Fence above the Sea* (2005). She is an assistant professor of English teaching creative writing at Clayton State University. She is also an editorial reviewer for *Confluence: The Journal of Graduate Liberal Studies* and writes microreviews for *Oranges & Sardines*.

purely practiced in hammocks, but by an urge to participate in a different kind of psychic energy than verse usually embodies."

I am interested in transcribing the workings of the mind. I am interested in writing the present of the mind, in the present moment. I am not talking about automatic writing here because my work is carefully constructed, but I am talking about constructing a poem from the multiple thoughts that assault my/one's mind during these mystical moments. We have all heard of a writer entering the "zone" in order to compose, which is really a trance-like state, though not the kind of trance in which your eyes roll in their sockets and your body shakes. It is rather a state of hyper-awareness. Rimbaud saw the poet as a seer and a shaman, which means he thought the poet capable of altering the very nature of reality through a sort of induced dissociation of one's personality, what he called a "reasoned derangement of the senses." This temporary state of mind is essential to my composition process because it allows me to tap into my subconscious, to reach my core, to go with what I call my "obsession" of the moment. I explore this "obsession" from all possible angles in each one of my books and know to abandon it when I reach the end of the book (or maybe it abandons me).

I wrote *Fence above the Sea* after I had witnessed the last week of my father's life in France. So you could say that I wrote the book from loss. After a long and terrible illness, he finally left me, his daughter, without a father. At the same time, I thought of being the mother of a daughter whose father has sunk into alcoholism and vanished. I thought of being a daughter and being a mother who is forced to be a father to a daughter. I thought of living in America with a daughter without a father. I thought of living in America with the memory of my father as she lives with the memory of her father. I thought of repetitions. I thought of signs. I thought of colors. I thought in French. And there was urgency. There were voices. There was simplicity. There was absurdity. There was the prose poem.

When I started to write *Fence above the Sea*, I was reading Leslie Scalapino's *that they were at the beach — aeolotropic series*, among other books, and I fell in love with it. At the time, I was also reading Gertrude Stein and Samuel Beckett, whom I take as my second set of literary parents, the ones I found in the English language, my first set of literary parents being Marguerite Duras and Milan Kundera, the ones I associate most with my native French. For me the *aeolotropic series* embodies what the poet Russell Edson had in mind when he stated, "A good prose poem is a statement that seeks sanity whilst its author teeters on the edge of the abyss. The language will be simple; the images so direct, that oftentimes the reader will be torn with recognitions inside himself long before he is conscious of what is happening to him." Scalapino's *aeolotropic series* is just that. Indeed, I had also read Rimbaud's *Illuminations*. I had read Baudelaire's *Le spleen de Paris*. I had read Lyn Hejinian's *My Life*. I had read Rosemarie Waldrop's *The Reproduction of Profiles*. And I have read many more collections of prose poems since then, notably, *Gaspard de la nuit* by Aloysius Bertrand, who initiated the prose poem by drawing on the medieval ballad's form to express oneiric thus surreal, scenes in prose. The innovation resides in the fact that Bertrand's prose pieces are not poetic prose narratives; rather they are moods, impressions written in prose. They are prose poems.

It is hard not to notice the diffusion of the prose poem in literary magazines today. In fact, it looks like this emergence of the prose poem is surprising and important enough that editors have started to reserve special issues for it. For instance, David Lehman edited the anthology *Great American Prose Poems* (2003), *The Mississippi Review* printed a special issue on the prose poem edited by Julia Johnson (2006), and there is now even this anthology *The Rose Metal Press Field Guide to Prose Poetry*. So why this sudden ubiquity of the prose poem? I think that because poets are the product of a precise historical, societal, and political context, their work reflects a particular environment, which, in turn, influences both the form and content of their poems. Today, we live schizophrenic lives in the sense that we are constantly assaulted by outside voices. We can be reached anywhere, at all times. We are expected to check our phone messages and emails daily, all day long. We all work, sometimes more than one job, manage our writing careers (especially for most of us poets), and care for our families. We are constantly under pressure. We cannot stop writing. And there it is. Compact, controlled, melodic, polyphonic, lyric, heroic. The poem in a box. The prose poem.

I cannot escape the prose poem. I tried to reject it in *The Dazzling Land* since that collection is about schism and addresses the split that occurred between my countries, relationships, and identities. Since I firmly believe that the content of any work dictates its form, the shape of this book represents a schism in form and fluctuates between lineated verses and prose poems. I cannot escape the prose poem. I immediately had to go back to it in my third book, *Song of a Living Room*. These poems are written in a series. They build on one another. They flirt with fiction. They are built around two characters. The excerpt accompanying this essay is taken from this collection. I have now moved on to another project, and it looks like it will be another collection of prose poems written in a series. There is already a blurring of the sense of time and space. . .

⁓

POEMS
(How to Sink the Surface)
The night unwrapped in blue as scheduled and she was cold without his breath on her skin. He pulled a string of words from her mouth to weave a winter dress. There was no time to plant new ideas. He said *letting what is asleep become wakeful.* She did not hear blades of grass crash against her thighs like glowing waves. She did not swim across the howling garden like a running fence. She did not dive to find pebbles at the bottom of his heart. She stood in nakedness. There. A splintered tree. A whispering rock. An alarm call.

(After Contemplating Wintering in Water)
She sat with the sea on her lap in a cold room and a white nest grew in her hand. The sky was blue as usual since she staged primary pigments as a rule. There was no ant dancing on her arms and she warmed up to her role. She said *Show me your teeth.* He said *Shall I come at the same time?* Depending on the accuracy of the narrative it was possible for their words to have stumbled upon each other. Just like that. Just like another vaporous day in Georgia. Just like a yellow

house vanishing under red leaves. Just like a dog leaving bones at her feet. She thought of the sound of rain. She thought of his steps in the garden. She thought of nothing else when he opened his mouth.

Jeffrey Skinner

THE OCEAN OUTSIDE THE DOOR
A Few Transformations Brought to You
By the Prose Poem Laboratory

It's nonsense to believe we will ever lose the desire for stories. We'll even listen to the telling of a dream if the telling is good enough. What happens next: Of all possible bits of knowledge, the thing we most want to know.

When I was beginning to write poems one of my heroes was Russell Edson. I loved what he wrote, and after I had read everything he'd published I went to the library to find out more about him. What I learned astonished me: He lived in Stamford, Connecticut—my hometown! He was the son of a famous comic strip writer. I had passed by his house many times. I didn't have the guts to go knock on his door, though I wanted to, badly. So I sent him a letter with some of my poems. He wrote back. It was miraculous. He said something like, *You seem to have talent, but who am I to say?* I read that letter three hundred times. But then, I didn't know what else I was supposed to do about the whole Russell Edson thing, and turned to other matters.

I was invited with my wife to live in James Merrill's house in Stonington, Connecticut for a year. It happened that I knew Stonington and loved it, and I had even taken my wife there for an early anniversary dinner. Now we had children almost grown, and we were living in the house of a famous poet, free to do nothing but write. The town ended in a peninsula,

Jeffrey Skinner's latest play, *Down Range,* had its premier run in New York City at Theater 3 in October 2009, produced by DC Productions. His recent poems have appeared in *The New Yorker, Kenyon Review, Valparaiso Poetry Review,* and *Poetry East.* He received an NEA Fellowship in Poetry in 2007, and was a MacDowell Fellow in April 2009. Skinner teaches at the University of Louisville, and lives in that city with his wife and two basset hounds.

and Merrill's house was there, on Water Street, in the center of a quaint but still operating fishing village. On the roof terrace one could see water in three directions; there were foghorns and church bells. Fishing boats left early in the morning from the small harbor, and came back one by one at dusk. Friday nights there was a fish fry at the Portuguese Holy Ghost Society Hall.

The combination of freedom from everyday responsibility and the slightly unreal town made me feel I had found a knot of stillness around which the grain of time swirled but could not enter.

Merrill's house had been kept largely as he left it, with his furniture, knickknacks, library, and Pulitzer Prize—modestly framed and hanging on the kitchen wall—all untouched. Many of the most valuable books had been removed for safekeeping, but we were free to use the hundreds of volumes that remained. My wife found many treasures there, but I found only one: *The Book of Disquiet*, by Fernando Pessoa. This was a book of prose that combined elements of the essay, the memoir, the poem, the meditation, the novel, and a panoply of other sources, in a seamless voice so compelling, so searing in its inwardness, that I read little else the whole time I was in residence. Each passage seemed to bring me to a new realm of the self, a place I had never seen and yet recognized at once. It was as if Pessoa were guiding me through the rooms of a mansion I had just inherited. I would read only a little, and then read it again. And then I would write, and what I wrote was prose—prose poems. The pieces were varied and fluid and the ocean filled them. I was delighted and inspired by the pliancy of voice, as the pieces gathered to themselves jokes and philosophy and rants and descriptions of landscape and memories, and dozens of other bits of consciousness I could not have found before I came to Stonington, to Mr. Merrill's house and library.

For me the prose poem is capacious and interior. Like a mirror, it holds as much as the world it reflects. I love to step inside. Things are a little strange in there, yes. But you don't have to stay in that one room, or even that house. You can keep walking, and find all manner of thing. The ocean, for example, is right outside the door.

efore my father died, I began to make poems in which he and I were characters in a fairy tale. The landscape varied but often I had to help him, or he helped me. I did not want to write the usual dying parent poem, with hospitals and descriptions of troubled flesh. Besides, it didn't feel that way. I had worked with my father in his business for many years, and whatever problems we had accumulated over the years had been largely worked out. There was at last simplicity to the relationship that resembled those in fairy tales. The poems came each day, sometimes two a day, for a two-week period. I would write them in my office at work, with the lights off. In one poem I dress my father in a custom-made bear suit and air-drop him in a remote forest. In another he is a conductor on the New Haven commuter line. In a third I wheel him into a park, where he gradually solidifies, joining the other statues.

I know people who would say I was working something out in these poems. But when you come down to it, in the contest between psychology and poetry the former is absurdly overmatched.

The prose poem can be a comic operetta, or it can be a theatre for grief.

More and more I find myself reading "science" books. By this I mean primarily those books by scientists past their research prime, written to flatter a lay audience into an illusion of their own heightened intelligence. I especially like the ones on physics, with such sexy titles as *Quantum Enigma*, *The Fabric of the Cosmos*, and *God's Equation*. I buy them obsessively and, though I do read them eventually, have a stack of backlogged titles waiting for me at any given moment. What I enjoy is the way these books pursue ultimate questions about the physical universe to their logical endpoint and beyond. I have never been comfortable with time simply unraveling in a straight line ahead. I have long suspected the universe may be composed of consciousness. I have wondered at the relation between the distance between particles and the speed of thought.

Such concerns, when examined seriously by someone trained in hard research, set off in me a chain reaction of sentences. The prose poem seems particularly amenable to associative mediation. It is my version of the thought experiment. It is my language lab, with high ceilings and electrical charges arcing across the damp gloom, tables and racks of intricately connected beakers and glass tubing filled with colored liquids, expanding and condensing and boiling up clouds of new elements.

And so I amuse myself. It passes the time.

The prose poem is an Eastern European running down a dark alley. I'd say he wears a topcoat and a bowler hat. I'd say he hurries to meet a shady doctor who has promised to smuggle him across the border.

I'd say it won't end well. But who am I to say?

POEMS

The Experiment

I sewed my father into a specially designed, handmade bear suit. He was indistinguishable from a real bear, and yet retained the necessary functions of a human. I also provided a G.P.S. radio collar. Then I air-dropped him into a densely forested preserve. When I returned a year later I found he had mated with an Asian black bear. He and she and their two cubs lived a quiet life in a mountain cave.

After sharing a meal of berries and honey and wild piglets I asked to speak to my father in private. He led me on a path away from the cave to the edge of a cliff. *This view of surrounding mountains and rivers and forest is magnificent* . . . "Yes, it is," he said. "What, you can read minds now?" I said. "A small trick for a bear, as it turns out."

I thought this over for a moment; but it did not change my purpose. "Dad," I said, "it's time to go home. The experiment is over." He stared at me with his great, incongruous blue eyes and bear face, and said, "No." "Yes." "No." "Yes." "NO!" he said finally and swatted a nearby Douglas fir with one paw. The tree flew several yards over my head and came to rest in the snow, dirt trickling from its upended roots.

"It's been good to see you," I said, and rose. "Same here," he said and also stood, "but I think it best if you didn't come back." I agreed, and held wide my arms for a goodbye embrace. I could hear and feel the cracking of my ribs, which I consoled myself would heal completely in time. "Don't tell your mother," he said. "In fact, tell her I've died." "Well, you are dead, aren't you?" "Yes," he said, and scampered up the path with surprising agility, on all fours.

Many Worlds

A physicist proposes time does not exist, only an infinite number of dramas, grand or banal, in different locations: a Wyoming ant hefts a leaf and begins the blind trek home. Nancy nicks her thumb chopping arugula in Manhattan. Sheets of rain batter the empty head of a seagull hunkered down amid blonde grasses. A Sudanese teenager takes the first of nineteen steps toward a landmine he will, or will not, trip with his left foot. A star in a tri-folded galaxy sputters and implodes. And so forth, ad infinitum. I read about this while drinking a steaming hot Columbian blend on the day we call, for convenience sake, Sunday.

But if there is no time, I wonder as I take another sip, why do I keep needing stronger glasses? And, if time is to be summarily tossed onto some landfill, wouldn't we be wise to hire a caretaker, an experienced force to guard the perimeter? One would not want the Spanish Inquisition leaking into Stonington, for example, where I currently reside. And I do not like to imagine walking the frozen streets of Buffalo, New York, and bumping into myself at the age of two, bundled in my mother's arms as she hurries me into the hospital, my appendix burst, my time running out.

How immediately I bend the poor physicist's notion to my own fears and wishes. . . Why must I understand every idea in terms of myself, my own little life and death? In all probability I misunderstand him completely and do not, as usual, know what I'm talking about. I wish I could step outside, into one of the many worlds to the left and right of me. *The boy recovered, in time, and lived.* But if time does not exist then why, as I continue sipping, does my sorrow deepen?

Alexander Long

SOMETHING LIKE A MEDITATION

Kalamazoo, Michigan, fall semester, 1997, and I came upon the prose poem via, well, prose. Specifically, Milan Kundera's *The Unbearable Lightness of Being*. Or Woolf's *To the Lighthouse*. Or maybe "Molly's Monologue" that wraps up Joyce's *Ulysses*. Or all of Nabokov's *Lolita*. Whoever it was, it happened about ten years ago when I was a graduate student. As a self-identified poet I was resentful (or skeptical or something) that I had to take a Modern Novel seminar; to compensate, I signed up for two poetry workshops: one in received forms that Sharon Bryan was leading, the other in "free verse" that Bill Olsen was leading. It turned out that Kathleen McGookey was in one of the workshops. Class after class, Kathy would turn in these compact boxes of words that made their own perfect sense. They sang, shined. Class after class, I would offer Kathy written feedback, something like *Wow!* or *I don't get it, but I love it…*or the unforgivable *Have you thought about breaking this into lines?*

Toward the end of that semester, having completed a paper on Kundera, and desperate for something to turn into workshop, I took a "poem" in lines and collapsed it into one neat, little square. I still don't know why I did that. Perhaps I was struck with a momentary bout of audaciousness: *anyone* could write a prose poem. What was the big deal? Kathy did it so "effortlessly" all semester. You simply take a poem in lines and get rid of the breaks. Done, and done. For about ten minutes, I may have been pretty proud of myself.

Alexander Long's first two books are *Vigil* (2006) and *Light Here, Light There* (2009). With Christopher Buckley, he is co-editor of *A Condition of the Spirit: The Life & Work of Larry Levis* (2004). An assistant professor of English at John Jay College, CUNY, Long also plays bass and writes songs with the band Redhead Betty Takeout, and is currently at work on a biography of Larry Levis.

Then came workshop. And, of course, Kathy was the first to respond.

Immediately, she was able to see—and more importantly to *hear*—where the line breaks needed to be (only better than my version before I bastardized it). I wasn't so much stunned as I was *schooled*. By dissecting my "poem" and helping it along toward what it needed to be (in lines), Kathy proved at least two things: one can't "just write" a prose poem; and the prose poem is its own necessary and beautiful animal.

I didn't know it then, but I was hooked.

Just after finals week, Bill Olsen and I met for lunch. I was hungry, not just for some lunch but for Bill's assessment of my poems, so I asked him—I remember my words distinctly—"What's this prose poem thing?" Bill politely laughed, then sipped his coffee. He said, "Check out Steve Berg's *Shaving*." That was it.

About two weeks later Berg's *Shaving* arrived in the mail from an online bookseller. I couldn't, as the cliché goes, put it down. Which is to say, I couldn't write. Berg's prose poems sprawl for pages, meandering *seemingly* out of control. Berg's voice is wild, loud, shouting, *wanting* to listen…and finally getting there, sometimes with a distinct measure of tenderness. Berg's use of the prose poem form enables him to capture the secular and profane alongside the metaphysical and spiritual. It was serendipitous, I guess, that it happened to be winter break, January in Kalamazoo, four feet of snow everywhere. It was serendipitous that I had nothing else to do but learn the language of the prose poem. Serendipitous, and daunting. I couldn't navigate Berg's terrain.

And I still can't entirely. And I can't explain why I sat down one morning—a blue-black dawn rising over all that white—and didn't read a thing. I sipped some coffee, then went outside for a cigarette. Call it 6, 7 a.m. And then it hit me—I went back inside with a sense of purpose I still can't name. I wasn't possessed. I felt no distinct inspiration, no luminous epiphany. But I began typing words that somehow *needed* to include Kundera, Brubeck & Desmond, a painting by Andrew Wyeth, my upbringing and education in Catholic schools in the industrial "suburbs" of Philadelphia, and my friend B. who committed suicide five years before that morning I wrote my first prose poem.

I was young, but no longer audacious; I was cold and alone and undeniably in the presence of many voices…and maybe I was just beginning to *hear* how blind I was. Maybe that's what I heard: all I didn't know, couldn't yet see. So, I typed. Huge, unwieldy chunks of words. Transitions…what transitions? Line breaks…what line breaks? I ignored all questions and doubts. I don't know how, but something like a meditation within me surfaced. But for who, for what?

I did hit save, but I also did my best to forget about the whole messy thing.

Then, around that March or April, I got a letter from Christopher Buckley asking me if I had any prose poems. Chris had found a couple of "lost" prose poems by Larry Levis, and Peter Johnson, then-editor of the now sadly defunct *The Prose Poem: An International Journal*, was going to take them. Chris suggested I send some stuff to Peter, and "see what happens." Chris's letter wasted no time, words: "You got any prose poems? Send them here—. Pronto!"

Still unsure what a prose poem was, or could be, or needed to be, I wrote Chris back and included the thing I typed that one morning months back. Chris called me about week later and gave me a title—"Meditation on a Suicide"—and provided the necessary paragraph breaks and tweaks in rhythm, cutting out the excess fat all novice prose-poemers eventually need to find on their own.

That summer, "Meditation on a Suicide" appeared in *The Prose Poem: An International Journal*. My name, on the back cover of that edition, appears just below Larry Levis'. That fact is an affirmation I still don't feel worthy of. Besides, it was just the luck of the alphabet for that particular issue.

I'll take it.

I'll take it, too, because B.'s suicide had been bothering me for a long time, and not just as a poet. Suicide is as mundane as it is singular. It's as irreversible as it is repetitive. B.'s suicide, in particular, was for me as foreign as it was intimate. I had not really been able to write about it before. My lined poem attempts (both in free verse and received forms) had failed, partly because of the closeness in time (yes, five years), but also because lines, meter, and rhyme somehow simplified the terrible gravity of the event. I needed time and space. I'd had plenty of time. Not until I encountered the prose poem did I realize what kind of space was available to me.

Perhaps most importantly, I found my voice working less stringently and more naturally, with a newfound authenticity and confidence that a sentence-based rhythm not only allowed but required. The truth is I was discovering—during the very act of writing *and* years later—that this "new" form and my "new" voice needed each other. In fact, form and voice within the prose poem are not separate; they are seed and tree. The kind of prose poem I found myself writing—then and now—is not narrative, but meditative, balanced precariously by parataxis and association, borne by the associative jazz rhythms and riffs on the "head" I grew up with.

And I had grown up Catholic, as did B. My Catholic upbringing insisted that B. was now in Hell. I couldn't accept that, and still won't. I don't portend that a poem can get someone out of Hell. But I do know that one of the chief virtues of the prose poem, as I try to write them, is space: space for despair and beauty to exist side-by-side, and in a voice that can sound only like *me*, whatever that may be.

POEMS

Meditation on a Suicide

> *…if there is no difference between the sublime and the paltry, if the Son of God can undergo judgment for shit, then human existence loses its dimensions and becomes unbearably light.*
> —Milan Kundera

True enough. But, I still can't say how or why I would want to leave this world on my own terms.

Listening to Brubeck's "Take Five" doesn't take long, relatively speaking, and it never gets above the level of a quiet conversation, like those held in confessionals or movie theaters right after the lights dim. It's just piano, bass, and drums shuffling unvertiginously, and Desmond avoids the root all he can, his lines slipping like sunlight on a butterfly. Every time I put it on, I wait for the solos that take off, not like a wren, but a Harley or Mustang, a drunk Marine—something so American objects on shelves shiver, and then fall off. But it never happens. Maybe they were on to something with this resignation from their lives that were trying to go everywhere on four chords and five beats. But then again, they didn't resign; all they did was reject the fundamental union of improvisation, which was their lives, because they could. Like I said, I don't know. Don't trouble yourself with what it is I want.

We want to look at each other sometimes, the kind of look that's uneasiness laced with desire, or the other way around. Around here, they're unidentical twins, so it doesn't much matter. Right now, for instance, I'm looking at Andrew Wyeth's nude Helga, *On Her Knees*. After a while, I want her, and I'm almost convinced she wants me too, except she's been looking down at a pillow all this time and her face is as flushed as bruised peaches. Her hands are behind her. I can't imagine holding them enough to go through with it. The more I look at it, the more I see that she's never been comfortable with this. So without ever touching the skin behind the ear, or kissing all the way down the inner forearm, we've turned each other down. And all this "passion," which is how Wyeth described it, is timeless. No wonder she was looking away. There's nothing like anonymity suffused with passion for all eternity. It smothers, I think, and it leavens.

I think it's all about becoming attainable, and being unattainable because there was a time when I was a part of God. I was provisionally eternal, back then. I can't say for sure whether or not I liked it, but why wouldn't I? When I was seven, I told Father Donahoe how my week was going. After a cough, he gave me ten Hail Mary's and ten Our Father's. I kneeled there for forty-five minutes. My back ached. This was my privilege, to be cleansed as such. I was the last to leave chapel that day, and Sister Amadeus kept me after that to clap out the erasers, punishment for failure in small Catholic towns. I found out that taking the Lord's name in vain also involved singing "fuck-shit-damn, fuck-shit-damn" to the tune of "Three Blind Mice" to no one in particular. B. told me this. He walked me through shit for years. We were taught that God was in the details, that we were made in God's image. I know I'm wrong, but I sit down and try to figure out a way to become attainable to God again. Nothing, so far, has been deemed acceptable, or worked, for that matter.

B. grew up one town over from me. They're both unacceptable towns to be raised in, unless you're a Catholic, or at least Episcopalian. Even then, it might not do any good. When B. went and shot himself in front of St. Joe's, where we were baptized, the pigeons in the eaves flew off in every direction, like veins and arteries or the lines on a map. The sky held still behind all this. That was his way out, and I'll love him for it. I'd better because I'm scared to death for him. It is God's nature to reject what was once a part of him. So what does that make B.? Oh, not now Whitman. I still love you, but please not today. Every single morning, at 6:30, pigeons fly out of those eaves when Mrs. McMurtry presses the bass pedals on the organ with her feet, as if she were walking through mud. Every blessed morning, and, occasionally, when I hear that unseemly shudder of surprise in some pigeons' clutter of wings, I feel closer to the truth than anyone.

Noise

It's the man in front of me half-turned around and staring, not the woman behind me whose voice controls her, summons those around her to turn and take notice for a second or two, those who'd care not to listen, those who have seen her before, know her, know what's coming, what she has and brings: small sounds from her nose; loud ones coughed up; murmurs shouted; cigarette-husk; throaty scats and half-words: *oh, ooh, yeah-yeah-yeah, uh-oh*; full sharp words: *eat, yes, now*; laughs that could be cries, cries that could be real, pain and joke overlapped and thrown together, encircled and sickled through her. The man looks at her, back at me, then down to his checkbook, squelches a chuckle, rolls his eyes, mumbles something to the cashier, particulars inaudible and hovering, and I could tell you that I chewed him out then and there, that I laughed along with him, exchanging barbs, cruel comfort; I could tell you that the woman lifted a clear and pointed *fuck you* at the two of us, echo and swirl; I could talk about clarity and why it blossoms inviolably in everything outside us—couldn't I?—how it sounds like a cat clawing at the door, wind in the lindens, the ocean.

Kathleen McGookey

WHY I WRITE PROSE POEMS

It started by accident. While I was finishing my MFA, I had a demanding full-time job, not a teaching assistantship, that left me little time or energy to write. So, out of desperation, I got up at 6 a.m. and wrote three pages as fast as I could. This usually took half an hour. Then I closed my notebook, showered, ate breakfast, and went to my job. After several days, I'd go through the notebook and highlight anything that still interested me: images, word combinations, sentences, bits of narrative. These I'd copy onto a clean page, writing from margin to margin. Sometimes while I was copying, I added new material. I don't know why I didn't use line breaks. Maybe because I took fragments from a page that had margins. The question of line breaks never occurred to me; maybe I suppressed it because I didn't think I had time to consider it. But there was something satisfying about producing a solid block of text, and above all, I was happy writing.

I had heard of prose poems before I started writing this way, but I wasn't setting out to write them. I was trying to find my way to some language or subject matter that I feared my internal editor would shut down if I paused to think about what I was writing.

Because I was enrolled in a poetry workshop, I handed in my prose poems. I am naturally shy, so just being in a workshop was a stretch. And

Kathleen McGookey's poems, prose poems, and translations have appeared in over 40 journals and 10 anthologies including *The Antioch Review*, *Boston Review*, *Denver Quarterly*, *Epoch*, *Field*, *Indiana Review*, *The Laurel Review*, *Ploughshares*, *The Prose Poem: An International Journal*, *Quarterly West*, *Seneca Review*, *West Branch*, and *Willow Springs*. Her book, *Whatever Shines* (2001) is available from White Pine Press. She lives in Middleville, Michigan with her husband and her two young children.

a prose poem pretty much announced itself as different as soon as you looked at it. This is what some classmates said when they saw my prose poems:

> *I don't know what to say because I don't know how to talk about*
>   *prose poems.*
> *This poem looks like a coffin.*
> *Just what is a prose poem?*
> *This would be even more powerful in verse.*

People usually got stuck on how a prose poem looked. Maybe I would have, too, if I hadn't been writing them. Still, I felt a little annoyed. Of course, the discussion would eventually move beyond this. And my professor would often write on my prose poems, *I like this*. Plenty of people had helpful and interesting things to say about my prose poems. But those initial comments got under my skin. I've never particularly felt like an underdog or set out to write something experimental or subversive for its own sake. I had figured out a way to keep writing when I feared I would stop. So I kept at it. One of my theories at the time was that if you do something long enough, you are bound to get better.

Luckily, my instructors helped by telling me who to read: Russell Edson (who I had read once as an undergraduate), Killarney Clary, Charles Simic, Gary Young. These are still some of my favorite writers. And of course, reading helped clear the way, showed me examples, and helped me figure things out. I've had two breakthrough moments in writing prose poems, which will probably sound very insignificant. But here they are. Reading Clary's work helped me figure out that I could break a prose poem into paragraphs to pace it, sort of like how stanzas pace a poem in verse. Without reading Clary, I don't know how long it would have taken me to realize this. The second breakthrough moment happened only a few years ago, when my prose poems got shorter and more narrative, and my instructor Sharon Bryan suggested I use wider margins. Now I'm writing much smaller paragraphs. Simply changing the margins transformed my shorter prose poems in a magical way.

Even though I eventually quit my demanding job, stopped my three-pages-a-day routine, and finished my MFA, I kept on writing prose

poems. There's something about the form that I just love. For start-
ers, I love that the prose poem invites the reader in. Readers are sur-
rounded by prose every day: newspapers, recipes, instruction manuals,
The Polar Express. These are all made of paragraphs, which generally
don't intimidate. But just looking at a poem can make a reader wary.
So the prose poem looks unassuming. Kind of regular. A reader could
pick up one of my prose poems and not realize she should be on guard.
By the time she realizes it isn't an interview with Princess Fergie in *The
Ladies' Home Journal*, I hope she's hooked. Or at least interested enough
to keep on reading.

I like to play with sounds and repetition and toy with sentence struc-
tures, and tell a story through a string of images. For a while, I liked to
tell a story and leave parts out. Could I do this in a poem in verse? Prob-
ably. But what's interesting and fun about doing this in a prose poem is
that the form—the paragraph—implies I am going to tell a story, deliver
information, and then I don't tell the whole thing. I liked creating a dis-
jointed feeling and using the prose poem's form to amplify that feeling
of disconnection.

What I love most about the prose poem is what the sentence can
do when it stands on its own as a unit of rhythm. I probably sounded
geeky when I used to tell my students that I love playing with sentences.
But I do. I like putting long complex sentences next to short ones. I like
using fragments and exclamations and questions and one-word sen-
tences. I like to use repetition of words, phrases, and sentence struc-
tures to create music in my prose poems. This I couldn't do in the same
way in verse because line breaks would interrupt the music of the prose
rhythms.

And finally, I love its small, unassuming size. My prose poems tend
to be about two hundred words or less and I love reading prose poems
about that size. I love the little magazine *paragraph*, which published
untitled paragraphs; I love the magazine *Quick Fiction*; I love the smaller
size of Simic's book *The World Doesn't End*. Right now, I still don't have
time or energy to write. I'm home with my one-year-old and four-year-
old all day, every day, which turns out to be a much more demanding
job than the one I had when I was working on my MFA. Now I work

twelve-hour days most of the time, and most weekends, too. So it's even harder to find time to read or write, but a small paragraph? That I can certainly write.

POEMS

October Again,

and the maple's leaves turn fire-red, starting with a single branch. My garden's tangled with mildewed vines. No frost yet. My wristwatch ticks. You never meant to hurt me by dying. The neighbor's dog, mistakenly let out of the house, vanishes. My son learns the alphabet, the sounds the letters make. Ducks fall from the sky, bleeding, same as every year. The tall grasses, swaying in the window by the door, catch my eye and make me think someone has come. When I answer my son, *Yes, everyone dies*, he replies, *Not us.*

Wish

I demanded, when available, seven to eight theories of sleep, including the whereabouts of our dreamselves during waking hours: twice in the night I've fallen for the touch that lingered, the luscious kiss on my bare shoulder. I couldn't help dreaming it. Such a pretty story: in love like stuck in the mud. The weather inside my head got better when couples sat on green park benches in the rose garden. But the names were wrong. They didn't know a rose was no talisman. My wish was short—a blue mitten no larger than a thumb, no larger than a dime, a wish so small. And it rose into the air.

Michael Robins

A WOLF IN GRANDMA'S CLOTHES
Undressing the Prose Poem

When people start talking about enjambment and line endings, I always shut them up.
This is not something to talk about, this is a private matter, it's up to the poet.

—James Tate

For as long as I can remember, I've been snared by that first unveiling of the poem on the page. Foolish and obsessive, I want my sight fixed on an object of beauty, palpitations and lust, a kind of symmetry that's surely subjective and most likely false.

The shape of a poem on the page is a first meeting of someone I want to wed, no less seductive than diction, tone, or metaphor, each contained in the form. Appearances matter.

We dine, we pour another bottle of wine, we share the cab ride home.

~

I'm awakened by Charles Simic's *The World Doesn't End*, a star no less dazzling than the city that reflects across the river where I was born.

The prose poem rides a donkey through the gates and I am baptized in its fold: a block of sentences, a paragraph, the bastard child of the short form.

Over drinks, a friend suggests the selected poems of Russell Edson, a pleasure to his eye and soon to my own. A gift that suggests simplicity and ease but bears false witness: heartbreak rears its head in these strange and inventive poems, permeates each setting through prose.

Michael Robins is the author of the chapbook *Circus* (2009) and *The Next Settlement* (2007), which received the Vassar Miller Prize in Poetry. His poems have appeared in *Crazyhorse, Denver Quarterly, Ploughshares, TYPO,* and elsewhere. He was born in Portland, Oregon, and lives in the Albany Park neighborhood of Chicago.

I once was found but am gladly tossed into a splintered version of the world.

~

I load my Volvo with boxes and books for Massachusetts, parking grave-side half a dozen times along the way. Kate Chopin meets me in St. Louis, not far from the playwright Tennessee. For each torchbearer I offer some private word—the closest I have to prayer—half believing a voice might rise in response.

The prose poem is personal, tranquil where the fresh water meets the salt.

Unique in form, the prose poem precedes a destiny manifest, the gaze of Lewis and Clark as they descend on the Pacific shore.

In Gettysburg I read Millay to Marianne Moore, but can't place Millay at her Steepletop.

~

The prose poem adheres to discovery and revelation, letting the horses gallop free.

My impulse to steal the reins proves itself in the use of couplets, a pair of lines like two dark braids of hair, eye level, enticing from a distance.

A journey upstream from prose, but one that encourages concision and has, more recently, developed in my attraction for ampersands and pentameter, each offering another degree of measure and possibility.

~

I sit for a time with Bishop in Worcester, Massachusetts, leave a bottle cap and coins at Kerouac's grave in Lowell. Dickinson, home sweet home, at last.

Line breaks, for me, resist explanation, and silence—from which a poem proceeds and concludes—rules the conversation. This is not to say that prose is the sinking vessel from which I row: every rule should be undone, re-examined, and broken again.

Underlying every sweeping statement is an exception, often more than one.

~

I pause for Hopper and his wife overlooking the Tappan Zee, the lone painters among these visits with writers. I cross the banks of the Schuylkill before reading *Leaves of Grass* at Whitman's tomb in Camden, the surrounding trees carved by visitors through the years.

Sylvia Beach in Princeton. William Carlos Williams in Lyndhurst.

I stop counting lines and syllables when the poem pulls the bobby pins, loosens its shoulders from such a formal pose. Face to face with the paragraph, the reader doesn't abandon his groceries in the street.

The prose poem knows the rules but is, after all, unruly.

~

Someone suggests John Godfrey's *Where the Weather Suits My Clothes*. A chapbook really, but one that carries a torch and, for the first time, I'm persuaded to sneak out of line into prose.

Imitation more ego than lyric, my own confession more than Godfrey's elegance.

A seed poorly planted but nonetheless a fissure, a flourish in the concrete.

At the graves of Emerson and Thoreau I kneel behind a camera, not even a stone's throw in Sleepy Hollow from Alcott and Hawthorne.

I'm tempted headfirst into the lines and prose of Laura Mullen, Joseph Lease, and Lisa Jarnot. I'm drawn to Stevens in Hartford, visit Frost on the grounds behind a white church.

The resting stone of Millay down the winding path I'd passed before.

Undercurrent and aftershock, the poem multiplies to feed the hungry masses.

~

Nearly all of my poems enjoy an infancy in prose. Prose takes the early breath that I indulge, rising from my knees to spur the sound and sequence straight before honing what at first seems stubborn into lineated form.

A hedge freshly shorn. The fruit over time into wine.

And yet I'm smitten within the short prose of Sarah Manguso, the escapade of Matthea Harvey, a sudden joy of Brenda Shaughnessy. I give myself to poetry, naked the morning after, a slipper in the dog's mouth.

A pigeon among seagulls and a seagull among crows.

~

Eighth wonder, the prose poem drops anchor in paradise. Older than

Baudelaire but alive and well, that which ruptures both prairie and sail with the song of sirens.

You can fill your hearing with wax, but the prose poem commands attention.

Half mannered, half the hell with you.

In joy and in sorrow, in plenty and in want.

The prose poem rides bareback into the sun and the view is astounding.

POEMS

Still Life with Steam Engine

The first is recorded in Wales, the first turn of the century, the heart of a horse replaced by water, to bring the workers home. I invented the passenger train without passengers. It shuffled toward the washed-out track. The details exist because I've seen a photograph, I've had many dreams: the skull of a horse in the Syrian, the angled break in a bridge, the dangling in between. I invent a survivor, the nearly widowed in the shape of a cloud, the flat chance on a scalded tongue. There the hounds smell the shore, a diver searches the seamless water for a misshapen valve. Now I'm tracing the depth & density of skid marks: the broken tree, the blame, my few hobbies, a guardrail gone astray.

Still Life with Gravestone

You have to return the book, whether you've read it or not, though every face, even the dead & dying, seems more likely to take another inch from the sheet that curtains the room. People die every day: a radio poised over the tub, the piano that spins by a rope, disputes that find a cold resolve. Think *banana peel*. The skin loosens its grip, the veins map a branch across the instep. You can't mend the binding. You can't pay the fines or feed the thinning air. The meter will soon expire, so move along, move along.

David Keplinger

NO EASY OUT
Some Definitions of the Prose Poem

No coach would instruct his team to win narrowly for the sake of the fans' excitement. Most coaches I know plan the most predictable games they can. And while preparation, talent, and strategy are important to writing prose poems, it's still hard to say what one is, or whence a good one comes. Yet whether theory can or can't apply to parsing them, we somehow know good prose poems when we read them. What is the source of our pleasure? Do prose poets think about craft?

I remember one evening during the 1980 World Series. Our Phillies played the Kansas City Royals. Pete Rose on our side; George Brett on theirs. My father and I sat in the basement of our home in the Philadelphia suburbs. I had started to learn two positions in Little League—catcher and first base—the very two I now watched closely on the screen. Playing first was Rose, dubbed "Charlie Hustle" for his verve and unmatched enthusiasm on and off the field, while Bob Boone, a Philadelphia legend, caught.

At an insignificant moment in play, a pop-foul had occurred (I have forgotten who was at bat) at which Boone threw off his helmet and stood looking up at the ball soaring down. It was an easy out. But in the right hand corner of the screen some baseball magic was happening. Here came Charlie Hustle down the first base line, running to back up Bob Boone's imminent catch.

David Keplinger's book of prose poems, *The Prayers of Others*, won the Colorado Book Award in 2007. He's the author of two other collections and a book of translations (*The World Cut Out with Crooked Scissors* (2007), the prose poetry of Danish poet Carsten Rene Nielsen), and has won the T.S. Eliot Prize, as well as fellowships from the National Endowment for the Arts, The Pennsylvania Council on the Arts, the Soros Foundation, and the Danish Arts Council.

Of course, it was comical. Boone, a catcher in the World Series, the best of the best, would surely not flub that catch. But by the time Rose arrived at center screen, that's what happened. The ball dribbled out of his glove into the hands of the arriving Pete Rose. The crowd stood and cheered. So did my father. So did I.

"Without contraries is no progression," writes William Blake in *The Marriage of Heaven and Hell*, arguably the first collection of poetry to be written with segments of prose. His insight honors tension, friction between pairs of opposites, as the central engine of the text. While Pete Rose surely might have suspected his hustle was for nothing, he instinctively accounted for the unintended—Boone might drop the ball. His save of an otherwise undramatic foul-out was so contradictory and delightful it remains among the one or two images I still see clearly from that series. (Another is relief pitcher Tug McGraw's third strike against Willie Wilson, thrown to win game five and the series.) The release of tension found its origins in two forces. The first was that I knew the rules and what I should expect. The second is that the utterly unexpected (except in Rose's mind) had just occurred. As Mallarmé said, it was the intersections, the crossing of the unexpected with the known, from which the meaning came, not via any single fact itself.

A prose poem is not a failed verse poem. As physical comedy differs from repartée, the prose poem is governed by conventions fundamentally separate from lineated verse. The prose poem can be funny, but it needn't be; and it needn't be solely absurdist, surrealist, or symbolist, though we often think of the form that way. By abandoning the line, all prose poetry does this: it snubs its nose at traditions that preceded it, traditions that, incidentally, encouraged a rational chartering of emotional states (e.g., the rigidly crafted Elizabethan sonnet). Sometimes cavalier, even irreverent, the prose poem might just as soon turn self-effacing and Chaplinesque. A joke, whose prerequisites include comic distance and reversals, can also be told with pitiable, heartbreaking sincerity. The prose poem, too, is itself a model of irreverence, inconspicuousness, a view from the side, an open mitt expecting out of nowhere the arrival of a foul ball.

Growingly our contemporaries embrace the prose poem form. I look at a collection like Joel Brouwer's *Centuries* (Four Way Books, 2003) and note that even established verse poets, poets who have great skill in breaking lines, are also drawn to prose poetry. Matthew Rohrer's 2005 collection *A Green Light* (Verse Press) mixes prose forms with lineated verse. Rohrer's speakers stand in the wings, insignificant extras in a cast of thousands. Here is my favorite piece from that collection:

Disquisition on Trees

The book that says the President is a friend of trees is a book of lies! The President should read the one about the little mouse that drove a car and got his girlfriend pregnant and they had to fly a rubberband-powered airplane over a stack of newspapers. Not a tree in sight. Not a tree in the whole book. Another book that he might pick up casually could strip the veil of illusion from his eyes: pretty women, the unpleasant foot odors of. But that is only what it appears to be about. It is a book about how to have a big piece missing from your head and live.

Even a poem 10 lines in length must operate on many levels of consciousness. Its lines are imposing a pre-language kind of thought, one not quite fixed in the new brain (rhetorical concepts) or in the old brain (images, mytho-psychological, associative concepts), but somewhere behind them, in the reptile brain, in the rhythm and the will of the heart. Denise Levertov called the lines of a poem its pitch or melody. Lines cultivate nuance. Further, lines evoke tradition, or they can suddenly break from a tradition to emphasize a word, a phrase. Without lines, what is left to fuel the brief flash of a prose poem?

While my third book, *The Prayers of Others* (New Issues Press, 2006), is a collection of prose poems that began as eight-line, lineated forms in iambic pentameter, I disagree that prose poetry creates music in the same way verse does. Prose poetry is, foremost, a revolt against traditional music, the way the avant-garde departed from traditional patterns of jazz in the early 60s. The revolt itself becomes the form. I think of Miles Davis' *Kind of Blue*. With Davis you are continuously reaching outward, the music is a straight line into space, but those unfolding changes are its constancy; they nearly tether us to something known, something like home.

In jazz, the leap (the solo: a brief but central departure), commands the listener to ride, enjoy the ride, until the melody hooks back. What does a prose poem mean? What does a jazz solo mean? Revolt. Joy. Revelation. Nonsense. Play. The prose poem is a solo, having come from, and going back to its melody in the white space, its larger story. We ride this thing; enjoy the ride. As I wrote the poems for *The Prayers of Others*, I held the solo as my model. I incorporated three leaps into each poem. I would lead the reader in a certain direction, then leap away. Then do that two more times. The poems were all about 80 or so syllables long (with some exceptions). Because I trusted the leaps to maintain a sense of form, I began to write about stuff I never dreamed I would—anything from Nixon's pee to sentient pliers, to Nietzsche, John the Baptist, and the little paper boats I learned about in *Curious George*.

If we could classify it, the good prose poem would look a bit like this: the pop-foul caught by the wrong mitt; a solo out of context of its melody; the sad comedian effacing himself. Loss and delight cross paths there. The good prose poem is indeed a tension engine. But without the pull between urgency and irreverence, it's no more than a riddle or an easy out, barely memorable at all.

POEMS

I **stood too close...**
I stood too close to the lion cage and was eaten right up. My mother called and called for me. I left no trace above. I landed in the lion's gut, and the gut was melted butter; its kills strung high along the cursive of its vertebrae. When the lion breathed in deeply, they flapped. I named this purring.

I **was a fabulous...**
I was a fabulous city-state bedeviled by an earthquake and a war. You were my guardian in the temple. All the soldiers on their parapets had tumbled into the sea. They were turning into dolphins. Their penises shrank into feeble contrivances. Even you couldn't save them, who were off somewhere helping Achilles to carefully strap his sandals.

Kevin Griffith

THANKFULLY, PHILIP LARKIN WILL NEVER READ THIS

My favorite poet is Philip Larkin. I know that such a pronouncement is going to seem insane in the pages of a book devoted to prose poetry, right? I mean, first, Philip Larkin probably didn't even know what a prose poem was, God bless him, and, second, even if he did, he would probably not venture within two miles of one. He was a politically conservative formalist. Once, when someone asked him what he thought of John Ashbery, he said, "I prefer strawberry."

But bear with me. Larkin works for me because he offers up a challenge to the reader without being pretentious. That's the aim of great poetry. Take a look at Larkin's "Vers de Société," and you will see what I mean. The voice is that of a crusty old loner avoiding an invitation to a party. It's a funny poem, a smartmouth poem, but on a second or third look, the reader begins to see the mastery of the form, Larkin's command of meter, his mind-boggling, almost impossible-to-imitate rhyme scheme.

But what do those things have to do with prose poetry, you ask? Isn't prose poetry about the avoidance of form, about casting off the shackles of metered and even "free" verse? Well, yes and no. Prose poetry, like a good Larkin poem, pushes the writer and reader to the extremes of what poetry can do.

In a good prose poem, we expect that the poet will push the imagination in the same way that Larkin pushed form. Imagination is the key.

Kevin Griffith's book of prose poems, *Denmark, Kangaroo, Orange,* won the 2006 Pearl Poetry Prize. Poems from that collection have appeared on *The Writer's Almanac with Garrison Keillor* and in *An American Life in Poetry,* Ted Kooser's weekly column on poetry. He teaches creative writing at Capital University in Columbus, Ohio.

My favorite prose poem is David Ignatow's "The Bagel." And I know, I know, it's not even a prose poem. But it's a poem in which the speaker trips, rolls, and becomes a bagel. Ignatow's poem upholds the spirit, if not the letter, of the prose poem law. In no other poem that I have ever read does the speaker turn into a bagel. That's originality, folks. That's what the prose poem allows more than anything.

I remember from my days in graduate school that many, many poets believed there was nothing new under the sun in terms of topics for poetry. "Isn't all literature about sex and death?," they argued. Thus, for many, poetry—and fiction, for that matter—was all about style. No one seemed to mind that your poem or short story, like almost everyone else's, was about your failed relationship with your "lover." What mattered was how beautiful the lines or sentences sounded. It was all about words and syntax. Nothing wrong there. But I was always left wanting more. Shouldn't the best writing take us to unexpected places? Shouldn't the best writing allow us think things we have never thought before? What's the point of beating a dead lover, no matter how skillfully you do it?

All dead lovers aside, prose poetry matters because it serves as antipoetry. As supporters of the prose poem, such as Charles Simic, have argued, not only do the usual haters of poetry detest prose poetry; many free verse poets do as well. Such is the attitude toward any art that challenges conventions. A hundred or so years ago, people couldn't stand it when poems stopped rhyming in obvious ways. Now they can't stand it when poems don't have obvious line breaks. Yawn. The only thing that never changes is people's resistance to change.

But there is more to it than just the lack of line breaks. Prose poetry challenges the pretentiousness of much of the poetry culture these days. And, boy, do we need something that challenges pretentiousness. Sure, prose poetry can be just as obnoxiously unfriendly to the reader as any other kind of poem, but humor has a better chance in the prose poem. I would say that there is a much higher percentage of humor in prose poetry than in any other form, though if you ask to see my data, I have no hard numbers. But take a look at the evidence: James Tate = funny. Peter Johnson = funny. Russell Edson = funny. I could name a lot more, but why bore myself and everyone else? You get the idea.

And not just funny ha-ha, either, but often funny in a dark and absurd way. Prose poetry is not for the irony-resistant reader or the chicken-soup-for-the-whatever crowd. Imagine David Lynch working for Hallmark and you have some idea of what I'm getting at. Take Tate's fabulous prose poem "Distance from Loved Ones." It's creepy enough that it makes the reader relive the awkward atmosphere of the dreaded call home to Mom, but when you realize at the end that it is the speaker himself who is dying and not the whining mother, the truth of the poem hits hard. No one suffers more than Mom, even if we are the ones about to croak. The best prose poems leave you with the feeling that you would be laughing a lot harder if the poem weren't so true.

So the prose poem makes us laugh. But it also makes us think. You can philosophize better in a prose poem. I love paradoxes. In my opinion, some of the greatest paradoxical statements are themselves prose poems, though you often find them only in philosophy books. Consider this one: "I am the Barber of Seville. I shave all and only those who do not shave themselves." Who shaves the Barber of Seville? You cannot answer the question, of course, but poems are about the beauty of unanswerable questions, right?

I also love aphorisms, the tiniest of prose poems. One of my favorite prose poets is the aphorist James Richardson. Consider a few of his gems: "The best way to know your own faults is to notice which ones you accuse others of." Or "Some things are too stupid even to be wrong." When reading Richardson's aphorisms, you begin to realize that the problem with much poetry these days is that once a poem gets started, it just keeps on going. And going. A prose poet, especially the writer of aphorisms, knows when to stop.

Ralph Waldo Emerson called his journals and notebooks a "panharmonicon," a musical device capable of imitating any number of instruments and playing tunes in which everything is allowed. That's what prose poetry is for me, the orchestra of fleas, making a noise we recognize as music, but a melody unlike anything we have heard before.

POEMS

Furnace

For days now, the furnace repair guy has been trapped in one of the ducts. How this happened, no one is sure. One minute, he's inspecting the damn thing, the next. . . . And because of the war, a war that never seems to end, I might add, the authorities are too busy to rescue him. Somehow he has positioned himself so that his face looks up through the iron grate of the main intake vent under our couch. Sometimes we slide the couch forward and let the children drop crackers and sliced apples into his opened mouth. On certain nights, the children gather around the vent and listen to him tell fanciful stories about wolves, elves, and armless people. He needs to keep mentally sharp, I'll bet. I suppose that something will have to been done someday. Especially when we need to warm the house. But for now, we just have to get used to it—the smell, the snoring.

National Poetry Month

The parade was dull. The queen old, wearing a frumpy sweater against the cold. No candy. The marching band wore black, smoked cigarettes, and whined a lot. Some guy in a beard guided a giant balloon shaped like a question mark. While the hyacinth girl ran off with the mermaid, a language poet read his work in his native tongue, something he called "language." People learned something, though— you can't teach old rain new tricks. And don't look a gift book in the mouth. In fact, don't look at it at all. Of course, most people don't need to be told that. The month was long and cruel—as it should be. When the parade ended, someone woke briefly and was awarded tenure. People went home to watch television. The home team won in extra innings.

Beckian Fritz Goldberg

CRASHING THE PARTY
Going Home with the Prose Poem You Want

My engagement with the prose poem was born out of annoyance. Sometimes I'd read these strange paragraphs as a "lapse" on the part of the poet too lazy to craft a poem. Some had an element of absurdity that I could appreciate. Some seemed indulgent. Some merely a passage of prose without energy or what Robert Bly might call "psychic weight." I'd been writing in line breaks since I could write, and I was writing bad verse by the time I was nine. I'd spent decades since learning the craft of the poem. I had no idea how one came to write one of these anti-poems and view it as a work of integrity. I knew how to love good prose. I loved the language of Hemingway. I loved the language of Raymond Carver. I loved the exquisite timing of the prose in a Ron Carlson story. So I did know that prose could sing, I just didn't know how the prose poem achieved its voice.

I was well into my career as a poet and as a professor of creative writing and the prose poem seemed to be undergoing a renaissance. I'd made a few blind forays into the form and always came up short. I had no conviction and one needs conviction to write anything. So I decided to teach a course on the prose poem out of impish perversion and perhaps a growing intrigue with a form whose mystery I couldn't crack.

By that time I'd read some prose poems I did admire. And some that I

Beckian Fritz Goldberg holds an MFA from Vermont College and is the author of several volumes of poetry, including, most recently, *Lie Awake Lake* (2005), winner of the 2004 Field Poetry Prize, and *The Book of Accident* (2006). *Reliquary Fever: New and Selected Poems* is due out from New Issues Press in 2010. Goldberg is currently a professor of English in the creative writing program at Arizona State.

loved. The one I remember most vividly is Russell Edson's "The Fall." Here were sentences that moved and seemed inevitable. There was an elegance and simplicity, what Edson calls the "humor of the deep, uncomfortable metaphor." It struck the same chord in me that a poem strikes, so I knew then that a prose poem could accomplish the depth, the resonance, the physical satisfaction that any good poem or good short story could. But how? That was the question that spurred me.

While I was still preparing to teach the course on the prose poem, I had attended a panel at the 1997 Associated Writing Programs Conference at which Robert Bly talked about the prose poem as being "more accessible" and less intimidating to readers, that this was the age of the "sound-bite" and the prose poem was uniquely suited for the pace of our contemporary world. I know, of course, that most people do freak out when they see line breaks and immediately start hunting for symbolism the way their middle school teachers probably taught them. This may be a factor in the resurgence of the prose poem—at least the perception that it is more "democratic"—but prose poetry will never be as popular as a John Grisham novel.

There was a lack of critical writing about the prose poem at the time. I wrote to Russell Edson, who was kind enough to answer that he saw his poems as "fables," and I also heard that David Lehman was working on a book about the prose poem, but most of what I found was scholarly work on the French prose poem that spoke of getting beyond the "subject-object dualism György Lukács describes as characteristic of bourgeois thought," or "the importance of undecideability as an active structural principle." What?

I taught the course twice in three years without writing a prose poem, and felt like a fraud while my students were much less inhibited and wrote some fine examples of the form. Since the class was open to both poets and fiction writers, everyone's ideas about genre were challenged. In a way, experimenting with a new genre was like having been married for years and then suddenly finding yourself single again. You have to learn all over again how to date, how to dress, what to say, what not to say. You become enormously self-conscious about your table manners. And when do you get physical? How physical?

As I began to inhabit the world of the prose poem, I also began to understand that it went places that were unique to it. And, most of all, that it had its own sound, its own rhythm, its own engine. For me, I had to be able to hear it before I could write it, the same as when I write lyrics. I have to hear the sentences, the cadences, the movement, and it was different than when one relies on line-breaks for the pacing and the torque of syntax. During a visit to the university where I teach, Russell Edson remarked that once he has the first sentence the poem "writes itself" from there. It makes sense when you read Edson as his prose poems often begin with an absurd premise or a direct declaration that establishes both the tone and the territory of the piece. You don't follow "A man once married an automobile" with "seasons of mist and mellow fruitfulness."

I knew enough not to try to imitate. Though there is always something to be learned from that, you have to make the thing your own. I was still flying blind. But when I read Jean Follain's *A World Rich in Anniversaries*, his prose poems were lyrical and evocative and did not worry about the epiphanic closure of so many lyric verse poems, nor did they begin with the quick "hook" of an Edson prose poem. For instance, Follain's "She Stops Short…" simply begins in the middle of a scene and we don't know what made the woman stop short or what was said to her. Rather Follain's piece pays close attention to the table setting that the woman was engaged in before she was momentarily interrupted, and to the activities going on around her. What attracted me to Follain was that he dealt with time and with place, two of my obsessions. I began to feel that I had a right to write the prose poem—perhaps an odd way to think of it, but it was important for me to feel I had something to bring to the table. The key, I think, is to discover what you want from a prose poem, and forget what you think it is or is supposed to be.

One night, very late, from about 2 to 4 a.m. I wrote four prose poems in a row. They just seemed to recite themselves to me. I did not "think" them. I heard them. One of these, "I Wish I Were Mexico," was a poem about my father after his death that I'd attempted a version of in lyric form a long while ago, abandoned and forgotten. The prose poem was the poem. And that's when I was hooked. You write a prose poem when it cannot be anything else. It comes as a prose poem. This is a joy.

As I continued to write, I found that, for me, the prose poem moved quickly. It did not lend itself to the same sort of pacing a lyric might and the tools for slowing down the language, then speeding it up where needed, required a different aesthetic. Looking back, I think that reading Stein, particularly her ideas about the sentence and the way sentences build into a paragraph, was influential. In many cases it was a balancing act. I also need to complete a draft in one sitting. While I'm generally inclined to do this when writing a lyric, I am willing to pause or, when I hit a road bump, take a break. With the prose poem I have to have the first sentence and that first sentence sparks the next and the energy builds. I don't do well when I pause and think. I have trouble re-entering the rhythm. A prose poem is still for me the most evanescent of creatures. I still can't define it anymore than I can adequately define a poem, but recently a student of mine said for her the prose poem "is like the ugliest girl at the party who is having the best time." To which I say, *Party on*.

POEMS

I Wish I Were Mexico

When my father came back from the dead he came back as a smell. He came back as a bus passing comes back as a cloud, fumy and genie-like granting three wishes. He came back as a seaside town. He came back as the great parlor of fragrance thrown open by coconut. Meanwhile the bus was winding past Taxco, the child hanging out the window on a mountain road wanting to throw up. And when the bus turned and held itself mid-air the child died and someone else got on with her life. That's the one my father returns to because it's so simple. You breathe. And the bloom of gin comes back like a tree.

He Said Discipline Is the Highest Form of Love

All three girls were in love with their music teacher. At a lesson, he told one: You wear your heart on your sleeve. Then the other came in, dark hair parted in the middle like a black book. She had the longest most promising fingers, but he did not love her. The third girl did not come until the next day. In the night she dreamed that he spread his arms out behind her and then wrapped his left arm to hers holding the instrument, and folded her fingers so they touched the strings. His right arm crooked with her arm holding the bow. They were just one violin.

Every time she practiced after that she felt his limbs on her limbs, his breast at her back, like a man-shadow cast by her small girl body. An hour would go by like an arrow. That's what was hardest: what love did to time. The Brahms fell apart like a glass. His shoulders over her shoulders. Even when she grew up, which happened in a night, and was happy, she could still conjure him, this love skin. This whole petal of him.

When she came to her lesson the next day he tapped the lip of her music stand with a baton, tic-tic-tic, four-four time. She felt—a bit, a bit of his ankle in her ankle, and then the knee above that, floating. She wondered what he was like with the book-haired girl. She knew he loved those long fingers. Maybe that was enough. In time.

Arielle Greenberg

TICKING THE BOX
The Rules and Permissions of the Prose Poem Form

By nature, I follow rules. I never got detention, for instance. Something there is of me, to manhandle the line in the poem by Frost, that loves a wall—I have a side to my personality that wants organization: lists that can be crossed off, boxes that can be ticked, tidy little pencil cases and adhesive labels and all the accoutrement of categorizing. I live by my well-kept datebook. I like strictly holding myself to assigned word counts.

It is therefore surprising, to me more than anyone else, that I don't seem to have a handle on the poems I myself am writing. Not that I am not in control of them, exactly: More that I have no idea how they come to be what they are, or how others will see them. When I thought I was writing clear linear narratives, my workshop peers reported to me that my work was oblique and baroque. When I tried to be self-consciously "experimental," an avant-garde press told me that I was, on the whole, too narrative for its tastes.

It follows, then, that I tend not to be able to follow the rules of received forms. We've all heard the adage about how one can be liberated by the limitations of formal poetics, but in my own experience, I've rarely found this to be the case. I struggle so hard to complete every prescription of a certain form that I lose all heart and verve in the effort, and so does the poem. The only kinds of formal poetry that have ever reliably worked

Arielle Greenberg is the author of two poetry collections, *My Kafka Century* (2005) and *Given* (2002), and co-editor of three anthologies, most recently *Starting Today: 100 Poems for Obama's First 100 Days* (2010) and *Gurlesque* (2010). She teaches poetry at Columbia College Chicago and childbirth education in the community, and is currently at work on a book of first-person accounts of the new back-to-the-land movement in Waldo County, Maine.

for me are those that reward playing fast and loose with their own strictures: the ghazal, for instance. I was steered toward the ghazal in graduate school, by one of my professors, Brooks Haxton, who hoped the form might give shape to what someone else, a literary magazine editor, deemed my "center-less" poems. Or the form of sprung rhythm, which Gerard Manley Hopkins originated: Since he made the form up, I've felt license to improvise on his basic ideas and come up with my own version. I do okay with following the rules of forms I invent myself, and these are the formal poems I tend most toward writing: procedural, elaborate, self-imposed game-poems.

Prose poems are another story. Prose poems, for me, are the best of many worlds. They are formal poems that defy the very nature of formal poetry. They are solid blocks of text—dependable, accessible-looking little bricks—in which I am set free to be as fanciful as I like: My prose poems tend to be the ones that most heavily rely on folktale and dream imagery, as so many of the great, historical prose poems I've read do. They give me permission to be narrative or autobiographical. They give me permission to be non-narrative and inventive. They let me make poems that look like traditional prose, and they let me make poems with weird margins and blanks and other assorted surface oddities. They allow me to tell lies, to be abrupt, to be glib, to be wholly sincere.

I'm not sure I remember how I came to know that prose poems would so often be the answer to my writerly prayers. I was fortunate in that I came to contemporary poetry at a young age, so I think the very first anthologies I read had prose poems in them, thus making the form a welcome possibility I could explore. But I have to admit that I don't often notice whether or not a poem is a prose poem: that is part of the beauty of the form for me. A prose poem's form feels inevitable, like all good formal poetry's form should.

The literal, on-the-page shape my poems take is frequently something that happens in the revision process; I do not know going in how long the lines will be, or where the stanza breaks will occur, or if a poem ought to be a prose poem, until after the poem is written. I try to let the poem tell me that information. Looking back on the first drafts of the prose poems I'm including here, however, I can see that many of them began their lives as prose poems, so there's obviously something in them that knows they are meant to be prose from the outset.

My real commitment to writing prose poems, though, originates not in poetry at all, but in that other genre, fiction. I have an inherent inability to "arc"—that is, although I love writing through and about characters and voice and events and all that narrative stuff, I can't seem to *take* it anywhere. No one tends to move much in my poems: I'm too interested in the language and images to get anyone on their feet. So I'm thrilled when I find novels in which narrative breaks down, swirls, collapses, lifts off into outer space. In high school, I obsessed over one paragraph in chapter 13 of Toni Morrison's *Song of Solomon* in which Hagar's newly bought makeup spills out onto a rainy street: The prose, like the puddle and the character's mental state, starts to swirl into a blur in an array of product names. I obsessed over all of James Joyce's *Ulysses*, in which the genre/style changes from chapter to chapter: I am crazy about Ithaca, the question-and-answer chapter, and Circe, the one written in the form of a play. And seeing Ben Marcus read from *The Age of Wire and String*— complete with a bizarre, Andy Kaufman-esque performance art prelude—during my first year of graduate school altered the course of my poetry immediately and irrevocably. I am enormously grateful for any encounter with literature that makes me gasp, "You can do that?!"

I've taught courses on hybrid-genre literature, and in these classes I always say something grand and ridiculous like, "Hybridity is the future of creative writing! Writing that limits itself to one mode of being is inappropriate to this postmodern age!" And I partly believe that. I am excited by work that code-switches and border-crosses, work that allows itself to be messy or jumbled or beyond. I am excited by the ellipses-ridden utterances of Chelsey Minnis' first book *Zirconia*, by the late Theresa Hak Kyung Cha's mysterious and political *Dictee*, by James Tate's irreverent and laugh-out-loud-funny tiny story-poems, by Joe Wenderoth's foul and furious postcards in *Letters to Wendy's*. I am myself working on two prose-poem-hybrid book projects right now: The first is a collaborative "polemic" on the issue of homebirth, with my friend and fellow poet Rachel Zucker, which utilizes accretion and collage of little blocks of text as argument, memoir, oral history, etc., inspired by the recent work of

C.D. Wright; and the second is a serial piece about life with my young daughter that plays with the notions of flatness and the short short story as rendered so well in work I adore by Lydia Davis. Although I love me a good rule, I love even more the poems that break them, and in my own work and what I choose to read, am always hoping to be pushed beyond the labels I adhere to myself or the categories into which I fit.

POEMS

ORD

It's called the night, what I just broke into. Little pieces, little pieces of my love life scattered in the down below and I'm lifting away, from the oh are dee to the ay tee el, through the hail, through the sheer camp of it, the glassined office parks, the halved valentines I tarnish and wear to be safe and return to you, you who mums me, circum-scribes me, loves me high and dry.

I am tuned to the music of the pilots. They are saying they are ready. They are sending wishes into the wires. They are a world of boys, so I grip on tighter. I am swimmy with the milky stars. I am in orbit around my concerns.

Fellas, push the tin I'm on, make it go steady, like a girl with a pin. I have a darling, she's down there, the prairie that's flayed across with Xmas lights, and I'm up in this unholy orchard, departing. I couldn't ever resent her but oh she keeps my voice down low. Push me into this dark ocean, boys, away and away, then sail me back home.

On the Use of a View: An Essay

What matters of a view? A surface for the over of our briefest minuet? A wash of the lake for the flat blue wash of our eyes? I've never. I've climbed for hours, past the treeline, looked once, eaten with gusto my granola, headed home.

We live by the lake because how could you live where we live and not be able to walk to the lake? But months go by and we do not walk to the lake. We buy a beach token and never use it. We do not go once the whole summer.

Oh, "nature." Huh.

But the baby runs again and again to the plate glass window in her great-grandmother's bedroom on Cape Cod. *Water,* she says. *Boats* (though there are none). *Come,* she says, fetching us from the interior.

Mark Wallace

SPLIT
Seam and Abyss in the Prose Poem

The prose poem is the most basic example of mixed-genre writing. It's a response to the earliest division made in human societies between types of language, that between prose and poetry. The prose poem always hovers near the site of this original division, although mixing genres does as much to create new genres as to blur distinctions between old ones. The prose poem: a genre whose possibility was created at the moment when genre was born, although it took people more than a few centuries to get around to it. A genre that marks the problem of genre even as its own history of genre markers develops.

It's not surprising that in studying genre, people have debated whether the prose poem is part of the genre of prose or the genre of poetry or its own genre. The debate is as inevitable as it is boring. An inexorable logic follows from the desire to categorize.

Not that I'm usually thinking about that when writing a prose poem. When I'm writing one my mind is most likely to be fixated, and frustrated, by the attempt to make the rhythm work. There's no doubt that for me at least, no rhythm is as complicated as the rhythm of the poem without line breaks. Some prose poems take me years to finish even when they're only a few lines long. In contrast, the line break feels like a signpost, even a guide, one that finally becomes, in the open field poetics

Mark Wallace is the author of more than 15 books and chapbooks of poetry, fiction, and essays. *Temporary Worker Rides a Subway* won the 2002 Gertrude Stein Poetry Award. He has co-edited two essay collections, *Telling It Slant: Avant Garde Poetics of the 1990s* (2001), and *A Poetics of Criticism* (1994). Most recently he has published a short story collection, *Walking Dreams* (2007), and a book of poems, *Felonies of Illusion* (2008). Forthcoming in early 2011 is his second novel, *The Quarry and the Lot.*

of Robert Duncan, a whole page and world of possibility on how to shape language. To me the prose poem is a kind of cramp.

I like to tell myself sometimes that the difficulty I experience with prose poem rhythms results from the complexity of my musical ear. It's comforting to think that when I can't get the writing to work. When you struggle with something like the prose poem as often as I have, it can be a boost of self-worth to think you're struggling because of your own ability. Obviously from the outside that conclusion looks questionable, but sometimes as writers we tell ourselves things that make it possible to continue. The prose poem is a crucial site of the lies I invent in order to keep going.

What to make of the fact that some crucial early practitioners of prose poems, Baudelaire and Rimbaud especially, are obsessed with death and decay? The link isn't accidental. Of course the connection between a subject matter that defies bourgeois norms and a form that challenges conventional literary distinctions has often been discussed relative to the prose poem's creation. It comes into being at the axis of writing about things powerful people don't want to hear in a way they don't want to understand. But its social and political condition also connects to my sense of the crampedness of the prose poem and its proximity to originary divisions. If for human beings the most crucial division may be between life and death, and the original genre division is that between poetry and prose, then matters of life and death must lie very near to what makes the prose poem. Anyone taking up the *violation* of the prose poem comes quickly upon the materiality of the body and peoples' ability to destroy each other and everything else. The prose poem sits close to the rot.

Still, it would sentimentalize similarity to think of the divisions of genre as wounds, and given the prose poem's specific history, it hardly makes sense to think of it as an attempt to heal wounds. Genre divisions are not simply the enemy of mixed genre or other innovative writing. It's too easy to suggest that any kind of "labeling" is unfair. As Ludwig Wittgenstein and Michel Foucault and Charles Olson and many others have suggested, limits are also creative, for better and worse, allowing human activity to take shapes that enable some possibilities while repressing others. I've often suggested that genre categories are useful guideposts to the morass of literature. It's when we see them as absolutes that the idea of genre becomes damaging to engagement with writing. Probably anyone who has taught prose poems at introductory levels has experienced the paradigmatic moment when a student, engaged or resistant or confused or hostile as the case may be, asks "But why is this a poem?" One answer is that it doesn't matter. We can talk about what the work does without reference to categories. Another answer is that it's a prose poem, a genre that mixes poetry with prose, and that the genre itself has a history, at which point we can return to talking about what the poem does with reference to those elements that seem like either prose or poetry. A third answer is that the prose poem questions such genre distinctions and raises issues about the human desire to distance, categorize, and control rather than engage. We can look then at the piece in terms of the way it resists easy categorization into prose or poetry. All three answers have been useful to me depending on the moment and the student and the others in the course.

Yet while the prose poem still contains this very basic potential for transgression, because people not overly familiar with poetry nonetheless recognize that it's doing something wrong, we live by now in a time when, pushing two hundred years after its creation, the prose poem has been elaborated into any number of contexts and niches. It's possible to write a narratively conventional prose poem and to write one that disrupts narrative or representation. It's possible to write one with conservative or radical or ambiguous social information. I have been fascinated recently by the translations by Don Mee Choi of South Korean poet Kim Hyesoon in the collection of Hyesoon's work *Mommy Must Be a Mountain of Feathers*, some of which are rendered as prose poems. However related to the original texts not included in the book, the prose poems come across as abrasive, often shocking surrealist narratives in which images of daily life in Korea have been transformed into dream-like psychosocial landscapes while the sentence structure remains relatively conventional. If one was determined to categorize: a Korean feminist daily life surrealist narrative prose poem. At least in translation. Choi's translations of Hyesoon make me think of Derrida's point about the infinite divisibility of the trait, the fact that all objects can be broken down into further smaller categories until finally any object exists only in its own category. The prose poem is a generalization.

I often have the history of the prose poem in mind when trying to write one, although that history can feel close to irrelevant in the intriguing and uncomfortable instant of struggling to find a word, of trying not to be overwhelmed by the distance between writer and language. I've always been a restless questioner of genre. It could be that I like undermining categories because I find them too comforting. At times I'm working on no more theory than that while around me the histories of categories rear themselves into the sky. The prose poem is a genre for those who either love contradictions or can't deny or escape them.

I don't dislike writers who work solely within a single genre, even the most conventional ones. Experimental writers can be too quick to issue wholesale condemnations of conventional genres. They fail to acknowledge that genres allow for an elaboration of technique, nuance, and understanding. Yet genres create structures from which to view and recreate the world whose limits no doubt are not always useful to everyone, and certainly not to the most wildly divergent ways of seeing. What we understand is shaped by the way we try to understand. The structural ambiguity of the prose poem always calls to mind the importance of looking and living through different structures and of questioning the structures we most believe in. The prose poem is a disorientation that allows for new orientations.

A mixed genre, a genre that marks the problems of genre, a cramp, a site for lies, a border between life and death, a violation and a rotting body, a ground for discussing technique and transgression, a history of niches and a generalization, a contradiction, a disorientation that orients while reminding us of the need for disorientation: In all these ways and others, a prose poem is a prompt and a possibility, a limitation and a goad, a site of engagement for the energy we have in the short time we have it. And even if I'm not thinking about all those issues when writing a prose poem, they remain essential to the challenge posed by its enigma.

POEMS

from Party in My Body

The hat sits on a pile of papers as if they're going out in the cold. Theories of who should touch us and why. From fairy tale to traffic nightmare, some thrill to the chill of first flakes, but ice stops travelers in their tracks. Why does the age demand nothing? Am I transcendent or drunk? People flutter in doorways and demented angels are ripe for a fall. All the things to choke on! If this looming gray building makes use of poetry, can poetry be to blame? When people hurry to work, it's not because work will vanish but because they know it exists without them. Gnash your teeth in an empty office and sing as though rebellion is here.

~

What kind of mind does it take to pull oneself out of the muck? In the sun, a row of small white crosses. I know this isn't the last jubilation, bodies pushing against the unknown. Is that a pit in the middle of the road? This symbol mixes sperm and blood in one more teasing crucifix. How people become bosses! All these monks have studied the classics. Shall we invent a melodrama and cast it with a dubious night? Is that poetry down on its knees, pleading with the producer? Close and close, far away.

Maurice Kilwein Guevara

PROSE POEM ELECTRIC

I wrote what was probably my second prose poem, entitled "Good Friday," in early 1989, at the age of twenty-seven. My first marriage was blowing away. The poem is less than a page long, oneiric, ekphrastic, epiphanic, soulful in a youthful way. A woman is flying over a small town, carrying a male figure above a rural Midwestern landscape. As to sources, I remember consciously trying to write close to the imaginative and imagistic aura that I had marveled at, a few years earlier, in Sherwood Anderson's *Winesburg, Ohio*. I also deliberately had in mind, both imaginatively and iconically, the print of a painting by Marc Chagall entitled *A Mid-Summer Night's Dream* that hung on my wall in those days when I was a graduate student living in Bowling Green, Ohio and Milwaukee, Wisconsin.

This lyrical poem became part of my first poetry collection. A more successful poem, however, "The Yellow Borges: An Answer to a Question" appears in my second collection; it's from the point of view of an imagined, ornery, blind Jorge Luis Borges as he answers a personal question posed by a group of literature students. The poem is butterflied down the page and seems somewhere between verse and prose. Partly historical, partly fictive, imagistically at once creamy as orchids and dismal as a coal-generation plant in winter, the work employs the labyrinthine psychological architecture one associates with Borges or

Maurice Kilwein Guevara was born in rural Colombia in 1961 and raised in Pittsburgh, Pennsylvania. He is the author of four books, including *Autobiography of So-and-so: Poems in Prose* (2001) and, most recently, *POEMA* (2009). He is a 2009–10 Fulbright Research Fellow in Ecuador, where he is researching and writing a novel. He is a professor of English at the University of Wisconsin—Milwaukee.

the Alhambra or the vertical neighborhood of Las Peñas in Guayaquil, Ecuador.

By my third collection, composed between 1997 and 2000, I didn't want occasionally to visit the prose poem form as much as I wanted to dwell in it, unpack my paragraphs, make voltage of the gaps between sentences and poems, paint the side door a lovely, genital red. *Autobiography of So-and-so* would be written entirely in prose poems. Two self-imposed formal constraints: each poem would not be longer than a page in typescript and all would be laid out in paragraphs. Like the Borges poem of a few years earlier, I wanted to liquefy the borderline between the empirically historical and the fictive. I was also aware, however, that I did not want to write short short stories, which were then in vogue. (By the way, one piece in the book, "The Halloween Party," fails in this respect in that it is driven more by plot than by poetical considerations.) That is, these were to be poems in the sense of being lyrical, imagistic, mercurial, metaphysical, sonic (albeit less rhythmically conspicuous than verse), and subjective as the premonition of a penny in your mouth.

In Michel Delville's cogent, critical, and generous study *The American Prose Poem: Poetic Form and Boundaries of Genre*, he cites Roman Jakobson who distinguishes between two evaluative axes of writing, the metonymic and the metaphoric. The metonymic is context-centered, moves sequentially forward in time, is associated with narrative, and is imagined horizontally. The metaphoric element refers to aesthetic or poetic writing, is comparative, subjective, vertically situated, and draws greater conspicuous attention to the text. Both of these characteristics are generally present, to varying degrees, in any discourse.

What made the texts in *Autobiography of So-and-so* poetical, for me, was their privileging of the metaphoric, the symbolic, and the liberal application of parataxis or of unconventional syntactic or prepositional coordination. I was trying to suggest the ionic body flavor of memory where it intersects vertiginously at the nexus of myth and history.

As I started to make a number of the poems for that book, I had the experience of feeling that the narrative, sequential aspects were weed-like, choking out the lyrical and poetic. I found remedy through greater syntactical variety, foregrounding cinematic imagery and perspective, modulating voice, length, and surprise. I wanted variety; I didn't want to become a sort of Aureliano Buendía, making a series of identical little golden fishes. In this respect, I sought to be different from one of my early favored prose poets, Russell Edson, who for all his superb imagination seems to have spent most of his artistic career riffing on variations of the same familiar bizarre scenarios, many involving his trademark monkeys. I wanted to make not only little golden fish (or monkeys), but sunfish as well as electric eels, puffers, pregnant seahorses, and microscopic breaching humpback whales.

Even though the collection has a narrative arc and the feel of a miniaturist novel, the energy and surprise come from what I want to call the lyrical elements—here I associate the lyrical with the sensory enactment of an imagined, subjective experience—the story of a moment perceived. I began to explore and channel the electrical velocity that occurs between sentences (images/ideas) in a given poem. I want to posit in the next section that the prose poem may work, in some cases, more as a metaphysical circuit than does a poem written in lines.

At some level, readers and poets are curious about the structural differences between the prose poem and its lineated cousin. More fundamentally, they are hungry to discover the essential features of a prose poem. This is where things get lopsided because verse and prose poems share more tendencies in common than in opposition, and it is extremely difficult to apply rigorous and exclusive characteristics that apply only to one form and not to the other. That is, one is hard pressed to work up a definition of the prose poem that strictly obeys the law of non-contradiction.

Yes, it's true that prose poems are written in paragraphs and not in lines. In this sense, the prose poem lacks the sonic (and visual) dynamic of the line break and is less conspicuously rhythmic than most lineated poetry. Of course, contrary to Charles Baudelaire's famous letter to Arsène Houssaye introducing *Paris Spleen*, prose poetry (or prose generally) is not without rhythm because rhythm naturally attends language, whether orally or in writing. Prose poems, more precisely, lack the secondary rhythmic layer of the line break and the systematic application of formal rhythmic patterns.

The developments that Delville discusses in his monograph (the ornate poetic prose of the Decadents, the epiphanic prose of James Joyce, the syntactic and perspectival innovations of Gertrude Stein, the plain speech patterns of Sherwood Anderson and Kenneth Patchen, the Deep Image examples of Robert Bly, the fabulist and surreal poems of Russell Edson and Charles Simic, the theoretically-informed practitioners associated with *The New Sentence*) do not necessarily point to exclusive characteristics or techniques that apply only to the prose poem, and Delville says as much. Russell Edson writes twisted, often hilarious fables that show us the grotesque underbelly of contemporary domestic life, but the worldview revealed in Edson's work may tell us more about the author's literary imagination than about his choice to frame his fantasies in what we call prose poems. Although Joycean epiphanies are often a feature of many contemporary prose poems, they may be even more frequently associated with verse.

So let me end this brief meditation by hazarding a guess.

It seems to me that the formal and receptive effect of a lineated poem is that it tends to be more linear than a successful prose poem. This may seem self-evident. The poem implicitly asks for the reader's attention to be focused on the line, which acts as a secondary syntactic unit with attendant semantic value. In this sense, the line of a poem is akin to the shot in film; there is greater chronological and syllogistic potential inherent in the formal structure of the line. The line is accrual by nature.

As much as this may be self-evident, it is also somehow counterintuitive as well in that we tend to associate prose with narrative and narratives with sequential chronicles and with expository transparency. Of course, from Laurence Sterne through Kathy Acker, those traditional notions associated with the representation of time in prose fiction have been periodically challenged and revised.

Lineated verse is deeply affected by the line as a syntactic unit in which context and content are realized (or extruded) in measured, linear ways by the author. (I'm aware that the current infatuation with anacoluthon as a compositional device immediately tests the limits of the case I'm making). In prose poetry, however, the line break is not available as an organizational unit so the writer depends instead on the sentence and the paragraph. It seems to me, for this reason, that some of the most interesting prose poems are constructed as complex electrical circuits with breakers and relays that create multiple patterns of energy and surprise in the gaps *between* sentences and paragraphs. In this sense, a well-made prose poem, when it carefully uses words and when it strategically does not, dramatizes the velocity of a human imagination at work and at play and in buzzing conversation with itself.

⌒⁑⌒

POEMS

Soup for an Oligarch

Using a cordless drill, stir the air in a clockwise motion until you hear trains where previously there'd been a swamp with lemon-soft birds and their graceless squawk. Keep stirring until the charcoal clouds over the pot begin to rain. Imagine a future in which you can see the features of your face arranged in the curling bark of towering trees corralling the entrance of the drained plot and park that will bear your name. Cut carrots and chives to the size of fingers. Avoid corn and tomato and plantain; use cilantro only if some shit-smelling so-and-so manages to press the nape of your neck with the cold-flat side of a machete. Otherwise, wear white turtlenecks and raise your daughters to answer either in French or in English. Above all, invest heavily in the miniaturization of pigs. When the gardener isn't looking, swirl your best cream into the pot and sprinkle with capers. Institute a network of radio stations. Play boleros and novelas. Play Chan Chan. Play Rayito de luna. Play Corona de lágrimas. Grind the orange-yellow flowers of a thousand zucchini fields into paste and incorporate slowly. To season with bromide, scratch the temples of your scalp. When the sows are small as beetles, toss a handful into the pot. They'll swim counter-clockwise for centuries in spite of the titanium ladle and the lightning and the waterspouts. Serve in bowls of polished bone in the many-mirrored dining room where even alone you are a multitude.

the other word for thesaurus

Is treasure. Or tesoro. For tesoro I mean the toddler who is in a body cast because otherwise his spine may become permanently deformed. I don't believe in God. Look at the bones of his shoulders. He is opening presents on his third birthday and says thank you but wishes the little book were a train named Thomas. For Thomas is another way to say César Vallejo. I'll talk now only if I can turn away. Say this in Quechua or Arabic. There is a dead man or teenaged girl in the mountains witnessed by roads. There is infinity in the skull small enough for beaks to enter. In the reflected stars we each touch the letters hidden there.

William Olsen

PARAGRAPHIC VERSES

If Walter Pater is right and poetry aspires to the condition of music, then does it hold that prose poetry is twice removed from the wellspring of poetry: song? This is to ask if prose poetry is any more removed from the sublime. Here, I mean sublime in the Longinian sense, which carries with it elements of the unsaid. Music, being non-verbal, fits this attribute. The answer matters not because of worries over the legitimacy of the prose poem. Not at all. It is a thriving form.

It is a form not yet thriving on codification and how-to aesthetics; it has not yet any theory to surround it. I don't know the rules, or even of the existence of any. One attraction of the prose poem is personal (attraction always is personal!): It frees a writer of poetry from expectations imposed by the sum knowledge of the craft of poetry.

If Pater's assertion is applied to the prose poem, it leads to defining the prose poem by an absence—of music. That absence has always inhered in the terms for verse and prose. Prose, from the Latin, literally, straightforward discourse. Doesn't sound very sexy. It's antonymical to *proversa*, which means "to turn." Hence Horace's notion that verse can be likened to a plowed field and the practitioner to an agrarian who brings order to the earth until it yields produce. Prose lacks turn, torque, dance, music, earthiness, diversion, cornucopia. The OED says prose is "the *ordinary*

William Olsen is the author of four collections of poetry: *The Hand of God and a Few Bright Flowers* (1988), *Vision of a Storm Cloud* (1996), *Trouble Lights* (2002), and *Avenue of Vanishing* (2007). His awards include a Guggenheim Fellowship and a National Endowment for the Arts Fellowship, and poetry awards from *Poetry Northwest* and *Crazyhorse*. He teaches at Western Michigan University and the MFA Program at Vermont College.

form of written or spoken language, *without* metrical structure" (italics mine). Like lowbrow art. Art without recourse to a sublimating music, the music of the spheres, the music in dance, the lute, the harp, the guitar.

Horace's analogy is comforting: assuming you own land to work in the first place.

I don't know how to explain intellectually why prose poetry has been in effect blackballed from canonical English literature for as long as it has. But open a *Norton Anthology of Poetry*: The closest work to a prose poem is from Geoffrey Hill's dense, allusive, richly historical, and, for all these reasons, intellectually authenticated *Mercian Hymns*. That's it. A few sections from one poem, from England's most aesthetically conservative living poet.

An active skepticism of prose poetry isn't practiced by other nationalities, and may have behind it some belief in the neo-Platonic notion of perfect forms—language put to flawless use, the absolute gliding invisibly forward and the words obediently in tow.

The opposing notion—that the prose poem is somehow closer to freedom and the common man and cleansed of artifice and of orders and of restraints and of structures that are hierarchical insofar as they can be ascertained at all—seems equally absolutist, dogmatic, dead-end. I see no greater urge in prose poems than in verse poems toward a given aesthetic—surrealism, naturalism, realism, post-structuralism—and I find in prose poetry no innate argument for the unconscious. I heard Tomas Tranströmer say once that the difference was that writing prose is like walking, with one foot on the ground at every moment, and that writing verse is like running, both feet off the ground a good deal of the time. This explains why writing verse can frighten me more than writing prose poems: I am afraid of heights!

~

Marcel Proust's lyrical prose—which changed my writing life early— flies unbound, and *because* of the sentence. It has as many aerial properties as poetry. The sentence becomes a vehicle of the eternal present, a grammar that relativizes events by passing them through an ever-revolving prism of the intellect. Or as Proust says of love, "space and time relativized in the heart."

~

The anecdotal prose poem, the allegorical prose poem, the confessional prose poem, the narrative prose poem, the surreal prose poem, the post-structuralist prose poem, the essayist prose poem, the absurdist prose poem, the postmodern prose poem: The prose poem is varied beyond any unifying aesthetic. Ah, but the writer rambles. To essay is to ramble. To ramble is to tramp off the beaten path. I sometimes think prose rambles, or strays, more efficaciously than verse: It isn't tied to return.

~

The prose poem's syntactic leanings are individual, even existential, and cannot finally be systemized. The long sentences of Stephen Berg's *Shaving* (Four Way, 1998) weighing possibility against the fate of Steve Berg, or the short sentences of Samuel Beckett in his great extended prose poem *Company* weighing possibility against fate: Pick your manna. I hear wonderful poetic effects in Killarney Clary, and I hear wonderful poetic effects in Lynn Hejinian. The former may preserve, the latter may disturb conventional syntax, but both use the sentence as an integral unit of cadence.

I observe a leaning toward description—sustained attention—distorted or not—in poetic prose. Even when the poetic goes abstract. In John Ashbery's *Three Poems* (Ecco, 1989) a rhetoric of description lends abstraction an almost painterly physicality: The intellect is arranged and deranged and rearranged—*canvassed*—all at once. . .

~

I loved discovering the pentameters in William Faulkner's *Absalom, Absalom!*; it was as if some civil war between poetry and prose were finally over.

~

Writing the prose poem can be a stepping down into something, a waking reverie, a dream in which the dreamer can change the dream while on a journey to inalterable realities. A descent, the old way, on foot.

I am now trying prose poems out as something other than strict prose, something that transforms without notice into verse, mid-paragraph, mid-sentence, something that syncopates prose and verse for the pleasure of the unique cadence of both, something that sometimes aspires to be prose, the song gone transparent. These pieces use line regulated by paragraph and sentence, and sentence and paragraph overrun by line. They could as easily be called paragraphic verse. Sometimes the sentence insinuates itself into song, and sometimes the song lapses into talking, and sometimes song and talk stop altogether.

There are gaps between bird songs. Birds cry territorially. Mostly, though, even birds keep quiet. Imagine instead of a bird as analogy for poetry—in verse or in paragraph—you used a forest, or a parking lot, a place made or created where many sounds can be heard, halting and persisting, at once, and where most of the physical world may be observed to be silent and even oblivious amidst all the singing and all the crying and all the listening.

～

POEMS

The Day After the Day of the Dead

A little sunlight every morning now, gashes of magnesium in graveyard clouds. Breakers blink on and off. Some days have as many as a dozen twilights and that many dawns and that many midnights and that many noons. Other days shake off sunlight in cascades until they have put off the burden of eyesight. And there are days of wind that are like years, and there are days that are like grass bleached to an almost dead language all at once stilled so that only the light can be said to move, and just barely. There are shorter days that are cinders, and even shorter days when the only colors are blue, green, gray, chalk, sediment, and chromium, as if the rest of the rainbow has been emptied into the kitchen sink. I have had days stare back at me as if to say, let's see who will darken first. For the strangest days of all are hemlocks in the midst of yellow beech. Their darkness is so alive that any light at all seems an insupportable belief, all so the blackest winter nights can have a place year round. These days are not only inevitable but possible, as old and fatal as childhood.

Voice Road

A ghost schooner of a moth crawling along night-black window glass soon to be defunct come the autumn blues that changing the heavens change all, stripping trees of their exhibitionist blush then even of their strip tease. And when night lifts like the underside of a dead bat curiosity turns over till certain its demise will exert no rabid influence and transform you into a posterity so vampirish it is unlivable simply to contemplate, then it is time to drag one's self up out of sleep, to haunt by being haunted by Voice Road, scenic drive all trees and sunlight-sworded open, road no more steady than this blade of grass the ant travels to the tip of the tip where no tip is and omniscience (non-existence) beckons, then crawling safely down its sojourn onto diamonded earth and coterminously along the lifeline of this paper confluences, so many cloudy clouds, so many met and unmet fiends and friends gathered wherever light of day, hearth, or deadflame lanterns reveals Masaccio's Adam and Eve banished not from paradise but from city, nothing to clothe them yet but anguish and shame for the only way to be in agreement with love is to disagree with design. Which is to say another fellow feeling seems out of sorts outside of Empire where Voice Road tracks as far back as ice-scratch, Bar Lake a glacial scion of a far larger glacial body of water, its glacial clouds, glacial trees, two icemelt lakes, one a sea, one a jewel, two temporary bodies temporarily separated by a gracefully interceding arm of dune, and where it is not bald, wind thrashed grass rooted in such sand-stung influence I would gladly suffer the joy of succumbing to a finalizing influence of elementalism to such drop-dead continuity, such gorgeously amorphous form, such merciful scattering, settling down, piling, hollowed out at the end of Voice Road, which says we shall be scattered all over creation. Though otherwise it's an ordinary road on which to rejoice crushed gravel, sand, glyphic tire tracks and mud-daubed leaves, impressions from the passage of lovers, friends, tourists, and locals who would be obliged to take any such conjuration of passage as this as lightly as a grain of sand in which the inhering gargantuan universal mass with a puff spirits away the place and the genius and the idiocy all pretend of emulating such kindly unaware, heartless, inhuman indifference in its unlasting forms clinging fast to some stability in instability.

Amy Newman

THE POEM IN THE GRAY FLANNEL SUIT

"Poetry's work is the clarification and magnification of being."
—Jane Hirshfield

When I had a job in Manhattan's corporate world, I'd put on a special sort of outfit in order to fulfill workplace expectations. I thought of my business wear as a costume that emphasized my singular focus and dedication to the clients' necessary tasks. Although inside the clothes I was a multitude of emotions, sensations, expressions, and music, to anyone who saw me I was straightforward, within the lines, full of gravitas. I used the costume to emphasize the distinction between the self I presented to the business world and my personal self. Photographs from those days record the external detail: I am all chemically-straightened hair, perfectly manicured long faux talons (we called them "power nails"), and sharp little suits that emphasized my aggressive business sense and expressed my familiarity with the hip graces indispensable to my field. But there was also a lot going on on the inside.

There are distinctions between poetry and prose, and there are similarities. Poetry's history is a history of the lyric voice, and prose's a story of the rational voice, less burdened by the soppy "distortions" of emotional song. Yet both are in language, the itchy tool we like to imagine may express both full sun and twilight. If I were a cartoonist I might draw poetry as a twisting, vivid heart inside active flesh, and prose as a series

Amy Newman is the author of *fall* (2006), *Camera Lyrica* (2002), *Order, or Disorder* (1996), and two chapbooks, *BirdGirl Handbook* and *The Sin Sonnets*. She teaches at Northern Illinois University and is the editor of *Ancora Imparo*, the online journal of art, process, and remnant.

of ruled lines in a notebook, and then a puzzled face: How does one put that flesh onto that lined paper, and then, how does one sing it? And I'd call the cartoon "A History of Writing."

The problem is that I am trying to locate a language art form that can unify the preconceived distinction between poetry and prose. While poetry is a distillation of idea through our sense of the world, it is not a private experience; as well, while prose is a tool to communicate information with clarity to others, such a distinction is limiting to what words can do. So we have something of a partition between poetry as song of the self and prose as the language we use to communicate.

It is difficult to pin down the imposition of this partition in historical time, but in the debate between Neoclassical ideals of reason and restraint and the Romantic counterargument of passion and wildness of heart, we can observe the categories as diametrically opposed: clear communication is rational, whereas the dreamy haze of our emotions is irrational. To serve the Neoclassical ideal of order, we would restrain this irrational element in our expression. To evoke our Romantic, emotional sense of the world, we would let the irrational breathe freely. These two have a tenuous, flirtatious, necessary, difficult relationship, and artists will try anything to get them to hang out in the same room for a while. The tension between the two is responsible for something specifically, terrifically human.

The argument between Neoclassic and Romantic was not just about the "proper study of mankind" but about the appropriate formal container for such study, distinctions between the cummerbund of tight heroic couplets and the unbuttoned blouse of blank verse revealing a preference for, respectively, the tidy beauty of a reasoning mind or the anarchic passion of the unruly heart. The mind does not deny the heart's existence, but which will be king of the body? Choosing may be less the issue than the belief, however inaccurate, that we alone suffer these contradictions and that they distinguish us from other species, elevate the human in and from the natural world. Thus the thinking/feeling man is further troubled by this feature, since it amplifies a feature that we take to be unique to our species and therefore essential to any representation of ourselves.

Consider the poetically informed distinction between birdsong and speech. Keats supposed that birdsong was perfection, because the nightingale sang out pure avian emotion unencumbered by the knowledge of the rational, human world. Such knowledge, with its sobering weight, would have dragged earthward the bright whistles. When a poet wishes to evoke his sense of the world, he must try to sound like humansong, which is—because of what we are burdened with, if we take Keats' word for it—more complicated than the sweet sounds of a clueless bird. If I speak sweet emotional birdsong in my poem, I run the risk of speaking in too private a language. Further, to imagine that birds are enraptured all the time has resulted in some very purple poetry. Whether or not it is true that birds don't bear the yoke of mortality, one thing is for certain: We are not birds.

A poem that so delights in its own emotional music at a certain point begins to forget the world of gravity in which we live. Yet with too much attention to the rational the poet runs the risk of speaking in our very public language, flattening out any aesthetic. Let's not forget Richard Hugo's declaration that once language exists merely to convey information it is dying. One element should not supplant the other. Is there any way to huddle the two opposing elements into the static shape of ink on paper fiber without flattening them? In the early twentieth century a gaggle of thinkers and artists conspired to invent a form that might evoke the multi-dimensionality, the vertical simultaneity of human thought, though they were forever hamstrung by the one-dimensional tool of horizontal sentences. But Keats too must have been concerned with the ballast of words, for he ends his ode in a twilight semifreddo, the mezzo addormentato of negative capability: *Hey—that bird I was so taken with…was it even here? Was I…dreaming?* The best of all possible forms would fuse these diverse poetic voices within us: confidence, hesitance, passion, gravity, and birdsong. And let the feathers fly. Such a form would embrace the depth and dimension of human perspective, a form with stereoscopic sight.

The brain knows what I'm talking about when I say stereoscopic sight. Art's responsibility, the re-presentation of what one perceives, includes both external details and how they are filtered internally through the

mind's eye in an unwieldy combo of thinking and feeling. Such percep-
tion and representation is a matter of "seeing"; we need only think of
Joseph Conrad's goal as a writer: "My task which I am trying to achieve is,
by the power of the written word, to make you hear, to make you feel—it
is, above all, to make you see."

If life were one-dimensional this would be a piece of cake—a flat,
one-dimensional piece of cake. But because of depth, Conrad's near
anguished metaphor concedes the difficulty of literal and figurative
perspective. Since Euclidean geometry we are aware of our binocular
vision, with the right and left eyes seeing slightly differing views: Depth
is a merging of the two. The brain amalgamates these parallax views into
one stereoscopic three-dimensional image. The delight of figuring out
how to more accurately represent depth—space in time—is not limited
to language arts. We need only to think of Giotto's apostles with their
flat, plate halos, Alberti's treatise on perspective in the Renaissance, della
Francesca's use of shadow, della Porta's binocular drawings, Chimenti's
stereo pairs: all attempts at revolutionizing form to represent the condi-
tion of depth in reality. Advances in art *and* in entertainment: Euclid's
recognition leads not only to the stereopticon and to Conrad, but also to
the Viewmaster you played with in third grade and those floating magic
eye posters that still hang in some banks.

I'm looking for the right metaphor for a language form that would
sustain the lively tension of what we take to be so uniquely human, a
form that would acknowledge the doubt in a fallen world at the same
time it allows for wonder. It must have structure *and* flexibility. Maybe
the prose form could be like a coat of armor within which the human
body may explore, equal parts protected and vulnerable. My term *armor*
seems so defensive, too archaic, with its parts of tempered steel: the gor-
get at the neck and pauldron upon the shoulders, gauntlet upon the
wrists, and on down—the cuisse, greave, sabaton. But I can't let it go,
because within that heavy, flexible container—a knight could mount a
steed, bear arms, battle, or run away—was a warm and living, thinking,
feeling human who could also kill, or die.

But beholding the knight's armor, might one immediately perceive
both aspects of the human condition at once? Beneath the glint and

through the visor's sight is no machine but a creature who doubts and wonders as much as he knows. The same may be said for me in my Manhattan days of Chanel and Escada, of Sonia Rykiel: such apparatus held a shape that didn't permit glimpses of my humansong, my wondering; I was there, in effect, but I also wasn't. What if there were a lithe language art that bundled together in its immediacy the rational and the irrational?

What if. Imagine what it would be like if any piece of generic prose—composition paper, a technical report, a cover letter—might be equally imbued by the natural and irrational voice singing into that prose template. What if the two could intermingle, the poetic voice inclined to visit the controlling gray flannel rational world of things, and the synergy so buoyant as to maintain them both? What if the poem and prose could party together and neither would regret it the next morning? The prose poem.

POEMS

Dear Editor 18 January

Gary L. McDowell and F. Daniel Rzicznek, Editors
The Rose Metal Press Field Guide to Prose Poetry
Department of English
Bowling Green State University
Bowling Green, OH 43403

18 January
Dear Editors:

Please consider the enclosed poems for publication in your anthology, *The Rose Metal Press Field Guide to Prose Poetry*. They are from my manuscript, *X = Pawn Capture*, a lyrical study of chess as my grandfather played it: the first move has to be made by someone who has not sinned. In this way the kingdom he created could be understood as a metaphor for family, and his fortress the dining room table, which he occupied until dinner, when my grandmother left off reading her calendar of saints, and brought in the platter of cabbages, along with her teary eyes. But I am saying too much.

As I am learning, poetry means to render as one renders anything; a boiling down to a kind of delicious syrup or troublesome glue, a thick liquid magic, like the manna oil, flowing from where the saints walked with delicate or tormented feet in life or after, when their bodies were free of indecisions. My grandmother reminded me of the miracle of the oil of St. Stephen when it made a dead man stand up and dance a kind of two-step of proof, and everyone's eyes watered and the crowd broke into applause, and the applause broke into doves flapping their wings against their hearts. In Bavaria the oil of St. Walburga flows out of a rock and is captured in a souvenir chalice, so that all may be cured of their terrible mortal leanings, such as when the boy from the football team tries to rearrange my blouse with his chin as I am pinned in his arms on those nights I walk home from a meeting, and I have been so embarrassed I can't say no. I have suffocated myself with fervent blessings and he still breathes his intentions all over me, so in my head I carry a treasure map of Bavaria, with a little cross for the church at Eichstadt where the relics of St. Walburga rest. In my version of the story the stone is a glassy green and the oils flow warm onto my pale forehead, and my body is relaxed among the turbulent wing beats of the gray impassioned doves.

Thank you for your consideration, and for reading. I have enclosed an SASE, and look forward to hearing from you.

Sincerely,
Amy Newman

Dear Editor 30 October

Gary L. McDowell and F. Daniel Rzicznek, Editors
The Rose Metal Press Field Guide to Prose Poetry
Department of English
Bowling Green State University
Bowling Green, OH 43403

30 October
Dear Editors:

Please consider the enclosed poems for publication in your anthology, *The Rose Metal Press Field Guide to Prose Poetry*. They are from my manuscript, *X = Pawn Capture*, an exploration of how attentive I was versus how wily my grandparents were in raising a tainted child. But if I *tell* you that I will have not *rendered*, which my workshop class says is something I must do. When I think of the word *render* I am reminded of how we get fat from our animals and boil it for seasoning; to take from their bodies the moist or succulent essence of them in life and transfer it, as one uses a metaphor, on to the pan or the onion or the bread. And when the bread of the flesh is rendered unto me on Sundays as a favor to my grandparents, I try not to think of St. Theresa who saw the Host only in the snapshots and leftovers He provided, and how irritated she must have been with her inability to get a clear picture and maintain the dimensional Lord in her apprehension of Him. Because how stubborn of Him to make it difficult for her and as a result she has to try in her own words to describe the experience and you know how frustrating that can be. How different the world would be if she'd had a Sony Ericsson Z500a© with its camera and 4x zoom to capture those minutes He offered her in the form of His Pale Wrist or His Muscled Thigh or His Bony Shoulder as well as (I'm imagining) His Heart Burning in Piety and she could have processed those snaps she had gotten, extracted the impurities from them and give them back to us, to furnish and provide, to restore us, surrender them so we could see, and these are all versions of *render*, which I am having so much trouble with, because such details as flesh and belief are tough to arrange as metaphor.

Thank you for your consideration, and for reading. I have enclosed an SASE, and look forward to hearing from you.

Sincerely,
Amy Newman

David Lazar

OUT OF MY PROSE POEM PAST
Using the Prose Poem to Enter the Language
of Films Noir

I'm not sure I can remember my first prose poems—but I remember the first prose poet I gave myself to, and that was Francis Ponge. I must have been twenty or so and stumbled across him the way I stumbled across most things those days: through a kind of accidental cross-referencing of books and bookstore shelves, using the former somewhat methodically, and the latter as a kind of carnival that I would get lost in and try to find my way out of, knowing that I would lose some innocence along the way. Those years of autodidacticism, before graduate school, before I had any idea that I could even think of being a writer, are very dear to me now. Reading and writing poetry were just something I did. And Ponge seemed so fresh, so archly Edenic. Take the simple object and describe it in blocks of short prose. Tell us what the object does. Its colors, the way it moves. Perhaps the object has several functions, or hardly any at all. Rain, a pebble, a door. "The rain I watch fall in the courtyard comes down at quite varying tempos" he tells us. And the statement hovers somewhere between the obvious and the revelatory, obvious because we realize the simple necessity of the statement as true, but revelatory because we realize that we're used to just seeing the rain as uniform. *Il pleut*. And that's why Ponge opened my eyes again and again. It was that knack for the small observation, sometimes wry, but never crossing the line of clever-

David Lazar's books include *The Body of Brooklyn* (2003), *Truth in Nonfiction* (2008), *Michael Powell: Interviews and Conversations with M.F.K. Fisher* (2003), *Powder Town* (2008), and the forthcoming anthology, *Essaying the Essay*. His essays and prose poetry have appeared widely. Several of his essays have been named "Notable Essays of the Year" by *Best American Essays*. He is a professor and the director of the nonfiction program at Columbia College Chicago.

ness that hooked me, and made me think that the prose poem was the perfect place for sentences that revealed what had been hiding, lurking in the edges of meaning.

My own prose poems are not all like Ponge's, but have extended this feeling into a noir sensibility. What is it in the sentences we speak that can become written sentences that reveal a fabric of loss and desire based on some earlier idioms and conventions of American film and literature? At least that's what many of my prose poems have struggled with. I have tried to take a language and extend it. Sometimes it's the surrealism implicit in the genre, or a more comical sense of the dark night of the American soul. Not in a Steve Martin way, but the joke-is-always-on-me existentialism of films noir.

Of course the best noir writing exceeded its generic pulpiness. Think Raymond Chandler, whose reimagination of American prose creates new pockets of partial self-knowledge, loss, and recovery, or the more self-knowing screenplays by Billy Wilder and Chandler for *Double Indemnity*, *Sunset Boulevard*, or Daniel Manwaring and James M. Cain's *Out of the Past*. I think I have Gloria Grahame's performance in the *Big Heat* so deep in my psyche that she shoots past my dreams just missing me.

The hard edges of the lost men and women of noir could still sing in sentences that hover somewhere between 1945 and the present. That's what I learned the more I wrote. I watched a lot of 4:30 p.m. movies, Late Shows, and when I couldn't sleep, The Milkman's Matinee. I'm dating myself. That's it, like a fossil or a piece of rock that some kid takes home and puts on a shelf. Noir is an American language of loss in aphoristic sentences. I loved it when I was a boy—it seemed hard and dangerous. And now as I see it as a language of loss, its hardness tempered by internal rhymes, and the pitch and pull of a short body of thought almost inevitably leads to a disastrous conclusion, though self-knowledge, and not infrequently a kind of tragicomic self-knowledge, may be part of the bargain on the way down. I've found the language of noir rather perfect for prose poems—tightly wound, perhaps one could say high strung. No chaser. Writing in film noir voices also connected me to the world of my Catholic neighborhoods in Brooklyn. Film noir, with its emphasis, on guilt, confession, taboo, was the perfect vehicle for a mostly autobiographical Jewish writer to explore what had been that taboo Catholic-attracted side of himself in voices that merged his own with those of men and women from his B-side.

Like many writers of prose poetry, what I also love about the form is its variety. A while after I discovered Ponge, I began reading Baudelaire, David Ignatow, Gertrude Stein, and Kenneth Patchen, but had no formal sense of prose poetry at all. I'm sure I wouldn't have used the term, nor did I start to write it until my 30s. I had by then been writing essays for years, my then confused poetry having succumbed to the delightful invitation to do the first PhD in the country in nonfiction with Phillip Lopate. But at some point I went back, found a film noir poem that just didn't quite work, and started, for some reason, typing it in prose. The result was one of the great lessons of form and rhetoric I've ever experienced. The cadences of the sentences, having lost their lineation, took on a rhythm between speech and metrical verse, but with no pattern of meter from sentence to sentence other than that of the character's speech cadences and accents. The improvement was severe, exciting, and I had been swimming in sentences already for years, believing that the essay could be built from prose that was as rich and dense as poetry.

In the years since that first, those first prose poems, I've gone on to write hundreds more—narrative autobiographical prose poems, prose poems that barely exceeded aphorisms, characters' brief monologues, surreal expositions—the form of the prose poem has such infinite variety, subject to the marvelous and sometimes excruciating demands (on the writer) of compression. But something about inhabiting those small complete worlds of prose appeals to me to no end. Both in reading (Rosmarie Waldrop, Eduardo Galeano, Amy Gerstler, Robert Hass, Lawrence Fixel) and writing one enters and leaves the prose, the poem, the piece, frequently with the propulsive sense of the escapability of acts and interpretations, but the need to think about them anyhow.

As the editor of *Hotel Amerika*, I've been pleased to publish prose poems by Galeano, Octavio Armand, Rosmarie Waldrop, Killarney Clary, Georges Godeau, Ray Gonzalez, Christopher Buckley, Gerry LaFemina, Tom Andrews, and other exciting prose poets, established and just starting out. I tend to look for work that stretches my sense of what a prose poem can do, rhetorically, and I'm biased toward a sense of musicality, except when the rhetoric is sharp and purposive. I like wit and distress to the point of extremis. As with the essay, I tend to be fond of pieces that resist closure. I have found that a fair number of prose poems that I receive ride heavy on conceits, and the danger there all too often is that the conceit merely plays itself out: short monologues of fairy tale characters, revisionist histories ("the real story of"), and anachronistic placement of literary characters ("Virginia Woolf at Disneyland") are the kinds of subjects that tend to play themselves out when not done superlatively.

But I think the prose poem still hasn't come into its own as an American form, and I suspect it is going to, soon. Journals are popping up that specialize in short prose. Literary magazines are publishing more prose poems. And very slowly, we're even seeing more books. With its polymorphous quality, sometimes fictive, sometimes nonfictive, highly poetic or philosophical, compressed and condensed, or merely short and written in relaxed aphoristic style (not an oxymoron), the prose poem is a miniaturist's dream of a form. And with our senses of attention constantly attenuating, the prose poem as the short form with most elasticity seems to have unlimited potential for writers and readers. Especially since it doesn't look like a poem. If some of the mainstream press, magazines like *The New Yorker* for example, would start publishing them, the audience for prose poems could be quite large. But for now, let's just enjoy the plenitude of *petit poemes en prose.*

⌒〃⌒

POEMS

Good Idea

I had one good idea in my life, and it turned out to be a bad idea. I sit at the window and watch the plans we made roost, leave their droppings, and fly off to God knows where. It wasn't just talk, wasn't just this and that and that and this, and boom boom we're in the money and the temperature's always 82, and your suits look like they were made for you, and not some monkey in Brooklyn. We thought about things, and we used our eyes. We had a guy inside who knew all the

dope and was married to somebody's sister. We made sure our watch-
es were wound and running at the same time. We slept well and re-
membered to leave our gaudy ties at home. We called our mothers and
said Hail Marys, loaded our gats, and even checked the tides. Then all
of a sudden it's like you're walking into a wall of warm air, your arms
get heavy, and you remember the one little thing that turns a good
idea into a bad idea, the one thing that you know you really knew, but
just didn't think enough about. Boom, boom, there's no money and
the birds might as well be heading for Capistrano, or any other place
where birds go to on their way to God knows where.

The Dark Lady of the Movies

I don't have to shoot. I don't have to glide words around the wound of
the world, or my own, like a schoolboy learning how to use a slide rule,
or something slipping down a dark alley. Men are terminally glib—
that's the original sin. When they rib you, you'd think they created you.
The rib is the rub; I let them think I'm amused. When I cross my legs,
or genuflect, I'm playing with two things I made all by myself—them
and me, like the monster making Frankenstein, and himself. I'm the
bride, but not Christ's, sugar, and not of any sucker in seersucker, with
a line in one hand and a little piece of shadow in the other. I'm the
bride of myself, a holy matrimony made in a hollow place near Sag-
inaw, and a ceremony where I play every part: priestess, bridesmaid,
bridesman?—I made that word up; I'm the woman who shouts her
own objections, the church in a red dress, the sacrifice of self-sacrifice,
a union of necessity and a torn piece of white linen. If you think you
see a streak of light across my eyes, it's because the face of the world
was conceived blackly, and a voice told me to provide something dark
and shiny, some image of self-image, repeated. I need an accomplice,
that's my fatal flaw, slouching towards a couch in a shabby room when
I should be the Empress of China, Cleopatra, at least Theda Bara. Even
though the asp comes out of my breast, it strikes back at its home;
but it's still a fatal mistake to think I won't get the goods on you, that I
could be shanghaied is a dirty little myth: I'm a hall of mirrors that no
one should ever shoot in.

Robert Miltner

BLOCKHEADS AND STANZAGRAPHERS

A stanza is an arrangement of lines of verse in a pattern usually repeated throughout the poem.[1]

~

A stanza is a group of lines set apart from the rest of the poem by white space above and below.[2]

~

A stanza, a unit in a larger poem, comes from the Italian for "station," "room," or "stopping place." When Henry Fielding was redefining the evolving English novel—a work in prose—he included chapters so his characters could stop in the spaces between them for the night, like lodgers at an inn. Rooms are square. Keep that image in mind.[3]

~

Paragraph comes from the Greek for "written beside," as in the way in which a beach is located beside a lake, or where a writer might construct a poem, that is, in a lawn chair on the beach beside the lake.[4]

~

A paragraph in the composition class is a group of sentences that support and develop a single idea. A paragraph can be one word, one line, one page or more, indented or not. It's any string of text that follows and ends with a hard return.

~

Robert Miltner teaches at Kent State University, Stark and in the Northeast Ohio MFA Consortium in Creative Writing at Kent State University. The author of twelve chapbooks and artists' collaborative books, including *Rock the Boat*, *Canyons of Sleep*, *A Box of Light*, and *Against the Simple*, his prose poems have appeared widely in journals such as *Artful Dodge*, *Barrow Street*, *DIAGRAM*, *key satch(el)*, *LIT*, *Pleaides*, *Prose Poem*, *Sentence*, and *Vox*. He edits *The Raymond Carver Review* and is at work on a novel, *The Tempest*.

A paragraph divides prose by emotion (Stein)[5] and by measure (Silliman).[6]

~

The paragraph, standing by itself, has a lovely pocket-sized quality, observes Naomi Shihab Nye, who adds, it garnishes the page, as a mint garnishes a plate. Many people say (foolishly, of course) they "don't like poetry," but I've never heard anyone say they don't like paragraphs.[7]

~

A verse paragraph is a division of poetry indicated by adding an extra linespace above and below the section to set it off from other parts of the poem. Unlike the formal stanza which is driven by rhyme, meter, or other poetic structures, verse paragraphs end and begin according to divisions of sense and subject matter, much like prose paragraphs in an essay. A verse paragraph sublets sections of the larger poem to other tenant ideas.[8]

~

Prose poetry is a new kind of flying machine, it's said Edson said.[9]

~

Prose poetry, Michael Benedikt told us, is a genre of poetry, self-consciously written in prose, and characterized by virtually all the devices of poetry.[10]

~

Prose poetry is a double helix. Since a prose poem is simultaneously both

[1] Qtd. in "Literary Terms and Definitions" at Dr. Wheeler's Website at Carson-Newman College, http://web.cn.edu/kwheeler/index.html.

[2] Qtd. in *Creating Poetry*, John Drury, Cincinnati, OH: Writer's Digest Books, 1991. 89.

[3] Qtd. in Drury, 89.

[4] *American Heritage College Dictionary* 3rd ed., Boston: Houghton Mifflin, 1993: 990.

[5] "Sentences and Paragraphs" in *How to Write*, Gertrude Stein. With Preface and Introduction by Patricia Meyerowitz, Dover Books, Books.Google.com/books. 30.

[6] "New Sentence," Ron Silliman. Originally in *Hills*, 1980; each is reproduced in numerous places.

[7] Quote. "Author's Note," *Mint*, Naomi Shihab Nye. Brockport, NY: State Street Press, 1991: np.

[8] Sentences 1 and 2 are quoted from "Literary Terms and Definitions" at Dr. Wheeler's Website at Carson-Newman College, http://web.cn.edu/kwheeler/index.html.

[9] Paraphrased from a talk by Russell Edson at the First Annual Prose Poems Workshop at the Great River Arts Institute in Walpole, New Hampshire, August 8–12, 2001.

[10] Direct quote from Benedikt, quoted by Peter Johnson in "Introduction" to *Sentence* 4 (2006): 13.

prose and poetry, the problem is a double problem, requiring a double solution. Twice as difficult, the risk; twice as satisfying, the solution. Imagine train tracks merging in the distance. Imagine paired skaters. Imagine lovers. Imagine yourself in the mirror.

~

The difference between a short story and a paragraph. Stein said. There is none.[11]

~

Stephen Fredman pronounces that prose poetry is the "last genre," since it fuses two of the basic categories of literature that have been divided since the time of Socrates.[12]

~

The distinction between "poetry" and "prose," saith T.S. Eliot, is very obscure.[13]

~

Prose poems, opines David Young, are life histories reduced to paragraphs, essays the size of postcards, theologies scribbled on napkins.[14]

~

Prose poetry is to prose or poetry as mongrel is to AKC pedigree. As shantytown is to gated community. As genre is to form. As fun is to norm.

~

The sentence to paragraph ratio, in prose poetry, is style.

~

The measure of divisible units in poetry is the stanza. In prose, it is the paragraph. In a prose poem, it's both the stanza and the paragraph. The measure of the divisible units in a prose poem is the hybrid stanzagraph.

---

[11] *How to Write*, Gertrude Stein. With Preface and Introduction by Patricia Meyerowitz, Dover Books, Books.Google.com/books. 30.

[12] Paraphrased from *Poet's Prose: The Crisis in American Verse*, Stephen Fredman. Cambridge: Cambridge University Press, 1983: 3.

[13] Quoted from "Prose/Poetry," Robert Alexander, *The Party Train: A Collection of North American Prose Poetry*. Robert Alexander, Mark Vinz, and C. W. Truesdale, editors. Minneapolis, MN: New Rivers Press, 1996. xxiv.

[14] Quote, re-arranged order: Young is quoted by John Drury in *Creating Poetry*. Cincinnati: Writer's Digest Books, 1991: 71.

The term is descriptive and will serve. And it sounds better than paranza, which evokes images of carnivorous fish in the Amazon.

~

When Aloysius Bertrand wrote *Gaspard de la nuit* in 1842, effectively launching the prose poem, he wrote stanzagraphs; when Charles Baudelaire wrote *Paris Spleen* in 1869, under the influence of Bertrand, he also wrote in stanzagraphs, in honor of that "famous" book.

~

In 1914, Gertrude Stein wrote *Tender Buttons* in tiny blocks. For her, "that is the way to pleasure a paragraph."[15]

~

Pedigreed dogs are beautiful creatures, within the limits of their breeds. Their value is in replication: consistency of line and look, predictability. Bred to stand there and look beautiful. Like supermodels. Like stanzas, like paragraphs.

~

When a mongrel dog gives birth, it is a surprise package, a spontaneous beauty, the prize in a Cracker Jack box, a thrift store find on fifty-cent day. Picture circus dogs, variety show dogs dancing in tutus, doing backflips, quirky and quizzing. Like stanzagraphs.

~

Stanzagraphs both orchestrate and emphasize the syllogistic movement of the prose poem, the interior logic that is the glue that holds a prose poem together.

~

A stanzagraph divides a prose poem in numerous ways.
By emotion, since a sentence is an interval (Stein).[16]
By measure, since emotion is a unit (Silliman).[17]
By disruption, fusion, or juxtaposition, since block is an expectation.

---

[15] Quoted from *How to Write*, Gertrude Stein. With Preface and Introduction by Patricia Meyerowitz, Dover Books, Books.Google.com/books. 28.

[16] Paraphrased from *How to Write*, Gertrude Stein. With Preface and Introduction by Patricia Meyerowitz, Dover Books, Books.Google.com/books. 30.

[17] Paraphrased from Silliman's "New Sentence" in Fredman, 196.

By form, since each poem is an organic unit with its own interior logic, by the shape on the page, by the frame of margins.

By intellect (Ignatow), to foreground the ideas that are at the origin of the artwork. Think of the way in which objects are placed in the three-dimensional foreground against the boxes. Imagine the boxes. Imagine the dimensions.[18]

By leap (Bly), in that the stanzagraph break in the prose poem block can represent the distance from which one thought leaps to another, the place we catch our breath before taking the leap. How else can the chicken cross the creek?[19]

By pace, both to establish or disrupt the prose rhythms of the sentences to work with or against a narrative thrust.

By action and gesture (Edson), the fusion or juxtaposition of the action that marks prose and the gesture that signals poetry.[20]

By making music without rhyme, the melody (poetry) and rhythm (prose) work together to give a prose poem sound, voice, character, personality, dimension.

~

Prose walks but poetry dances. Which is why a prose poem moves so funny on the page.

~

Many prose poets retain and rely on the "block" with its single paragraph and justified margins. Some call themselves blockheads.

~

No man but a blockhead ever wrote, except for money. Samuel Johnson said that. He also said that patriotism is the last refuge of a scoundrel. Such wise men deserve our attention.[21]

~

Other prose poets break their work into sections, like grapefruits or or-

---

[18] Paraphrased from Ignatow, quoted in Fredman, 8.

[19] Paraphrased from Bly, quoted in Fredman, 9.

[20] Paraphrased from a talk by Russell Edson at the First Annual Prose Poems Workshop at the Great River Arts Institute in Walpole, New Hampshire, August 8-12, 2001.

[21] http://www.samueljohnson.com/writing.html.

anges. Do they make the decision as prose writers, into paragraphs, or as poets, into stanzas?

Or, as prose poets, do they consider how the sectioning needs to consider the linguistic, grammatical, and formal structures of a genre that "blurs" the distinction found at the intersection between poetry and prose? If so, their work falls into that other category, the stanzagraph. Such prose poets are stanzagraphers, supple and rugged enough to adapt themselves to the lyrical impulses of the soul.

~

The first and most important point is that, in written literature, poetry is normally typographically defined, observed Ruth Finnegan when considering its relationship to oral poetry.[22]

~

In a recent issue of *Sentence,* the one edited by Peter Johnson, there are an almost equal number of blockhead prose poems (68) and stanzagraphed ones (62); in *The Party Train: A Collection of North American Prose Poetry,* there are more stanzagraphed prose poems (167) than blockhead ones (103). That's just a sample. That's just editorial taste. That's something to consider.[23]

~

Paragraphs develop ideas through description, definition, details, process, comparison and contrast, classification and division, cause and effect, analysis, chronology, linearity, special organization, orders of importance, problem-solution, or narration.[24]

~

The purpose and effect of short paragraphs is often to provide transition to a new focus: shifting gears, redirecting the reader.

---

[22] First part of the sentence is quoted from "Prose/Poetry," Robert Alexander, *The Party Train: A Collection of North American Prose Poetry.* Robert Alexander, Mark Vinz, and C. W. Truesdale, editors. Minneapolis, MN: New Rivers Press, 1996. xxv.

[23] *Sentence 4* (2006); *The Party Train: A Collection of North American Prose Poetry.* Robert Alexander, Mark Vinz, and C. W. Truesdale, editors. Minneapolis, MN: New Rivers Press, 1996.

[24] Sentence one is paraphrased and adapted both from Diana Hacker, *A Writer's Reference,* 5th ed, Boston/NY: Bedford/St. Martin's, 2003: 26; and from Sally Barr Reagan, et al, *Writing from A to Z,* Mountain View, CA: Mayfield Publishing Company, 1994: 284.

~

Stanzas can make a poem more inviting, according to John Drury. Their white spaces offer some breathing room, a stopping place or station for the reader. Small units are easier to read than a monolith of text. Like the difference between a haiku or Proust. A studio or a suite.[25]

~

Unity occurs when every sentence contributes to the development of the idea. Disruption, half-brother to disunity, occurs when they don't. Or when the contributing sentences from what would be a solid block of prose occur in other stanzagraphs within the body of the prose poem: that too reconfigures our ideas of unity. Non-disruptive prose poems rarely make history.

~

Coherence allows readers to move easily through the paragraph, following the writer's idea as it develops; such coherence is achieved through single point of view, one tense, one person (I, you, she), appropriate transitions, conjunctions, and juxtapositions, parallel structures, pronouns with clear antecedents. Pedigrees and thoroughbreds have coherence as they stand there, looking pretty.

~

Enjambing the prose block with multiple ideas disrupts the readers' expectations, offering a less predictable and more enjoyable text. Back-flipping, frisby-catching, bungie-jumping and hood-surfing: those prose poems are crazy. Wild form, man, Kerouac used to say.

~

Blockheads or stanzagraphers, let's call the whole disagreement off. The two can tango, hiphop, electric slide, or boogaloo: it's the miracle of poetic prose, Baudelaire would say, musical without rhythm and without rhyme.[26]

~

---

[25] The first three sentences are direct quotes from Drury, 90.
[26] "To Arsène Houssaye." *Paris Spleen.* Charles Baudelaire. Trans. Louise Varése. NY: New Directions, 1970. ix–x.

POEMS

Schism

He wore his skin like a shell. He kept another skin inside, the difference between bark and bite, smoke and fire. He knew the questions long after everyone's answers.

One day, he reached down into his throat and pulled himself inside out, sock-like, sack-like, right in the street, his internal works exposed like a busted watch.

Many ran away in fear, thinking him an alien, but others called for seizure, locking him up as a lunatic. A few embraced him, calling him the messiah. They ran him for public office. They ran him out of town.

You Know What They Say about Pears

Frumpy, heavy-hipped, green with envy of apples, the pears wear babushkas and pull carts filled with celery and cabbage out past West 88th and Detroit. Grainy sweet like candy eaten at the beach, freckled in or out of the sun, a pear is the younger child all brothers and sisters watch out for but never want to play with. The sad pears— Bartlett and Bosc, Seckel and d'Anjou—cry themselves to sleep. They see themselves as teardrops, tongueless bells unable to celebrate, or quotation marks with nothing to say. In their dreams, they run away to Hollywood and become avocados.

Gary Young

THE UNBROKEN LINE

I remember picking up the Kayak edition of Robert Bly's book of prose poems *The Morning Glory* when it was first published in 1969. I was moved by the simplicity of the poems, their clarity, economy, and lyricism. I liked the way they sat on the page. I was an undergraduate at the time and hardly well read, but these were not the first prose poems I'd come across. I couldn't imagine that the short prose vignettes punctuating Hemingway's *In Our Time* were stories—I assumed they were poems, and still do. Anne Bradstreet's *Meditations Divine and Moral*, Walt Whitman's *Specimen Days*, and of course my Peter Pauper Press edition of *The Jade Flute: Chinese Poems in Prose* led me to believe, naïvely it turned out, that the prose poem was a common and an accepted poetic form. Looking back, there was a genuine blissfulness to my ignorance.

In college I was introduced to the work of Francis Ponge, Charles Baudelaire, and Arthur Rimbaud. I fell in love with Russell Edson's quirky fables, and I read the prose poems in Charles Wright's *The Grave of the Right Hand* and James Wright's *Moments of the Italian Summer* with admiration and delight. I considered the prose poem only one of any number of free verse forms available to poets, and I recognized the prose poem's value as such. When I published my first book, *Hands*, in 1979, a single, long prose poem served as a fulcrum for the short free verse lyr-

Gary Young's books include *Days* (1997), *Braver Deeds* (1999), winner of the Peregrine Smith Poetry Prize, *No Other Life* (2005), winner of the William Carlos Williams Award, and *Pleasure* (2006). His *New and Selected Poems* is forthcoming from White Pine Press. He has received fellowships from the National Endowment of the Arts, and other awards include a Pushcart Prize and the Shelley Memorial Award from the Poetry Society of America. He edits the Greenhouse Review Press and teaches at the University of California, Santa Cruz.

ics that dominated the rest of the book. There were no prose poems in my second collection, *The Dream of a Moral Life*, but while I was working on that book I was being drawn inexorably to the form, although I was unaware of it at the time.

I was experimenting with longer lines and longer rhythms, trying to write a poem of "equivalence" as I put it to myself. I wanted to negate hierarchy in my poems. I wanted to write poems with as little artifice as possible, poems that began and ended on the same rhetorical plane. I was fortunate that my work as a fine printer provided a confluence of this theoretical concept with its physical articulation on the page. I was printing an artist's book, *The Geography of Home*, a volume of relief prints stitched together with a single line of prose that ran for nearly 100 pages. This long typographic line served as a kind of thread upon which the many woodcuts and other illustrations in the book were strung. More importantly, it mirrored what I wanted from my poetry: a horizontal rather than a vertical structure, a poem that one might walk along rather than fall through. My subsequent book, *Days*, was composed entirely of brief prose poems, but in execution and conception I considered them to be very long one-line poems. Despite variations in length, I still conceive of my poems as meaningful utterances playing out upon a horizontal field.

The prose poem's democratic itinerary, its horizontal rather than vertical trajectory, engenders a resistance to hierarchy and to inflation. Its fundamental nakedness may offer solace, but within a block of prose there's no place to hide. Karl Shapiro put it well in a poem from *The Bourgeois Poet*: "This is a paragraph. A paragraph is a sonnet in prose. A paragraph begins where it ends. A paragraph may contain a single word or cruise for pages." It is this suppleness combined with a certain brazenness that keeps me working in the form. I have found it more difficult to lie in prose, either through omission or amplification, and the moral pressure the form exerts is well worth whatever I may have lost by abandoning stanza and line.

Although my last four books are comprised entirely of prose poems, I don't think of myself as a "prose poet," and I have become increasingly uncomfortable with the term. Language poet, confessional poet, new formalist, prose poet—I see little benefit to this balkanization of the art. It's true that I am a poet who writes "prose poems," but like most terms employed to describe some aspect of aesthetics, the label is convenient, but inaccurate, limiting, and doctrinaire. I am a poet, a lyric poet, and my fundamental project, like that of most lyric poets, is to stop time. Among its many virtues, the prose poem allows me to write lyrical narratives that hold within their knot of language a world, a whole story. Some poets exploit the prose poem for different reasons, and other poets will find nothing of use there. In any case, the poem will find a way, with lines or without, and whatever form is most conducive to the poet is the one that he or she should take advantage of.

Robert Frost once famously said that writing poems without meter and rhyme was like playing tennis without a net. One wonders what he'd have said about poems that have abandoned the line as well. With the prose poem you don't need a net; you don't even need a court. You just hit the ball as far as you can, and follow wherever it goes.

～

POEMS

The earth submits to seasonal drift. The stars slide, and the planets swing higher over the horizon every day. This morning the sun sent a shaft of light through a rift in the redwoods; it followed the steep angle of the canyon, skirted the stream, the wild azalea, the granite cutbank, and shined on the brick stoop beneath the stone arch at our gate. It rested there only for a moment, but my son found it. He sat there warming himself, and anyone watching the light play over his body could have believed he was made of gold.

~

I couldn't find the mushrooms under the begonias in the garden, then I remembered I had seen them growing there in a dream. The flowering thistle, dewdrops clinging to the spider's web—it wasn't all a dream. That's coffee I smell, not wood smoke; and here's the glass vial where my wife has saved all our children's teeth.

Nancy Eimers

JUST RUNNING
Open Landscape and the Prose Poem

Pierre Reverdy has a poem the title of which has been translated as "One More Explanation for the Mystery." That could easily be a description for the first prose poems I ever read. They were often surrealist fables, surrealist odes; this would have been in the 1970s. I didn't yet know about Baudelaire or Reverdy. In W.S. Merwin's *The Miner's Pale Children* I found an ode to knives, "those gentle creatures . . . who make no sound, except an occasional clear note like the calling of a bird, when they have been struck." In Russell Edson's *The Clam Theater* a man was arguing fretfully with an ape over morning coffee. Since then, every good prose poem I read seems "one more explanation for the mystery." What is the mystery? That reality, as René Magritte once said, is irrational? Each year I give my undergrad poetry classes a handout of as many different kinds of prose poems as I can find. Through the years I have found that the poems I include are different than the poems my grad students put on handouts to give their students. They know younger poets whose work I haven't read yet. The tradition, such as it is, goes on, by way of swerves and hairpin turns and backtracking and wormholes.

I ask each student, based on the samples I give them, to come up with a definition of the prose poem. This is almost a surrealist exercise in itself, as every poem on the handout is a definition in and of itself, one that contradicts all the others. I tell them they can freely contradict

Nancy Eimers' fourth poetry collection, *Oz*, will be published by Carnegie Mellon in 2011. Eimers is the author of *A Grammar to Waking* (2005), *No Moon* (1997), and *Destroying Angel* (1991). She has been the recipient of a Nation "Discovery" Award, a Whiting Writers Award, and two NEA Fellowships. She teaches creative writing at Western Michigan University and in the MFA Program at Vermont College.

themselves. My own definitions in response to the samples turned into a list, with as many items as there were poems:

> A prose poem chooses one feature or object and compares it to things it is violently unlike.
> A prose poem is a seduction.
> A prose poem is a fable about an irrational universe.
> A prose poem is a hushed, bare description of a dangerous moment.
> A prose poem muses on objects without which we would be nothing.
> A prose poem creates a portrait of someone with a profession that makes us distinctly nervous.
> A prose poem speculates on what is just outside the frame.
> A prose poem insists on the reality of a dreamscape.
> A prose poem insists reality is a dream.
> A prose poem tells a story about betrayal that ends with a message that can't be translated into any human language.
> When narrative begins, a prose poem jumps the tracks.
> A prose poem speaks of the hour in which we lie awake.
> A prose poem wakes from its blackout somewhere between poetry and prose.

I once saw Lyn Hejinian's *My Life* in the fiction section of a bookstore. Mistake or judgment call? I told someone who won a creative nonfiction award that her work felt like prose poetry to me. She nodded. "Don't tell the judges," she whispered.

Campbell McGrath has a prose poem, "Manitoba," about stopping at a gas station during a locust plague. It is as if within the space of the poem language keeps changing the rules, or maybe it is that different times speak different languages; in the lingering gas station moment time gets formal, almost Biblical, the locusts "primordial, pharoanic, an ancient horde of implacable charioteers." But the tank is filled, and in human time "it was time to hit the road."

In the wake the 2008 Kentucky Derby, after Big Brown won by five lengths and the filly Eight Belles came in second but broke both ankles and immediately had to be put down, there were many articles about the breeding of thoroughbreds. They are bred for speed and for short, intense careers. My friend emailed me, saying, wouldn't it have been great to be a wild horse, back before all this, just running? I tend to head instinctively into prose when a poem has become too much about line breaks or some insisted-on metaphor keeps shrugging its shoulders. There's something about the writing of a prose poem that seems to promise open land and distance in which you can lose yourself. (Sustained rapture?) Sometimes it's just good to have the illusion of being in a place without fences. Then you head out into it, it starts to change. The distance turns out to have all kinds of invisible obstacles requiring a leap or swerve, negotiation, a radical change in direction—it makes its demands on you, and maybe it turns out, after all, to be a poem, or something you hope might offer one more explanation for the mystery.

⌒ҹ⌒

POEMS

I Finde in a Boke Compiled to this Matere an Old Histoire

… reading my husband's starred copy of History

Measured by human reading time, they are old stars. Something that belongs not to the past but to us though I wasn't there yet. Left-handed stars, each begun and ended at its radiating upper point. Often the lines don't meet, the star stays open a crack. Or the line continues through itself just below the place it started and the star opens up again. I don't want to make too much of this, just everything. *Historein, historia. To inquire.* Greek and Roman and Midwestern history. Athens, Florence, Des Moines. *See Weid—. To see.* Sometimes a star nearly flies or shrugs out of itself, sometimes there's a pock at the first/last point, where the pencil first hit the page or where it lifted off, which was it, twenty years ago. "Almost 80 of the poems in *History* are new," Mr. Lowell is quoted as saying on the back of the book. Before we went inside the house on Hol Hi Avenue, we wanted to buy it just because it bordered on a quiet with trees. And because of the name of the street. Once inside we didn't like the house; we adored the view.

View, vista, vision are some important derivatives. *Survey, idea, history, story.* And *penguin* from the Welsh *gwyn—white.* The page of my Jane Austen was filled with snow, the only sound the clinking of her bracelets. Where I came from you don't write in your books. He is part of his time, she is part of hers, though time gets dark at the top, I can't see into it. It's OK, I can hear him in the kitchen chopping kale exactly now. No, it is the smell of onions drifting to me. *Evident, interview.* Entre, between, plus voir, to see. A history isn't windows and trees. To write truly the history of last week, we would meet, some he and she, light years ago in Des Moines, Witmer Pond, put our bodies on in a light wind, put on all they have to say under one of the trees, open the book—not the trees, don't carve names on them—and start writing all over it.

Photograph of a Young Girl, 1941

1. You know the one. She looks up smiling from the book she is reading. She could not have been reading the sentence I just read by Virginia Woolf: *Every day includes much more non-being than being.* Woolf wrote this sentence in April 1939, two years before the looking up from the book, the smile. But the sentence hadn't been published by then. Woolf died in 1941, and the sentence stayed inside her handwriting, in its past. "A Sketch of the Past." You know the one.

2. She is wearing a watch. She is flirting, really, with the camera, or the eyes on the other side of it.

3. If this were biomedicine, we would be studying a photograph of her eye, so magnified it would give an anatomy lesson: lacrimal punctum, lacrimal caruncle, semilunar fold, gray line, lacrimal lake.

4. We see into the black and white of her, which is something else. A Ferris wheel through fog. The shadow of snow geese passing over but not in the picture.

5. She knows who is taking the picture, we don't, it's simple, she smiles, it must be someone she likes or wants to like her,

it must be a relief not to be studying, the watch on her arm doesn't weight it down, time is simply the time it is on her wrist, nothing worse, a moment of being, and maybe, considering how alive she looks, the next minute will be one too, and the next.

6.   The blank pages of the book are so bright they almost pour up from themselves.

7.   A book I am imagining to be about light, about the degree of value between black and white. If she woke from her life, she could turn the pages for us, a book of photographs. The close-up of a bullet. The mournful eye of an elephant almost lost in its puckers of hide. The lunar surface of a horseradish. Mottlings on a grain of rice.

8.   *I feel that strong emotion must leave its trace; and it is only a question of discovering how we can get ourselves again attached to it, so that we shall be able to live our lives through from the start.* She, Virginia, wrote.

9.   Would she want to (Anne)? Live her life through from the start? *Our baker's boy got hold of some sewing silk, 0.9 florins for a thin little skein, the milkman manages to get clandestine ration cards, the undertaker delivers the cheese.* She, Anne, wrote. By now she was in hiding. Writing was being. Non-being—the long nights? The ultra-quiet days? The being—sounds in the warehouse by night, everyone using the wastebasket for a toilet—the non-being, not being able to flush the actual toilet with workers downstairs by day?

10. Looking up, does she even remember reading? Isn't that joy on her face, maybe the joy of just lifting the head?—movement that abandoned its photograph. If this were not her face but a cross-section of her hair and skin on a slide, the longitudinal filament would be telling us it is not the hair of a mouse or sable or an Indian bat as we look down through the eyepiece of the microscope.

11. Her hair is black. Each shaft as she sits there in living time tugs up blackness out of the light—

12. A word is not remembered, it is not even lost. On the cover of her own diary she is looking up, *my* book on *my* desk, straight up into nothing, the ceiling, smiling, from the book *she* was reading. Or change the emphasis: smiling *from* the book she was reading, because of?—having taken it in. Into the light and fog of her. Look. There are rows of poplars in a flooded field rising out of themselves.

Joe Bonomo

HYPHEN
Sketching the Bridge with Invisible Ink

The lyric moment has always held the power of narrative and the heft of a story. My long-held admiration and love for *raconteurs*, for friends or stumbled-on strangers who can command the energy and attention of a crowd with a detail-spiked story, casts my own limitations as a story-teller into clear relief. The ebb and flow, the conscious climb up Freitag's Triangle, the deforesting of the brambly tale up ahead—whatever metaphor works for you, it never worked for me. *Your stories are great!* I'd say, but never while looking in the mirror. I was too self-conscious, too ego-driven (too ungenerous?) to lose myself in a story while leading others to a satisfying end. This may be why I felt compelled to write lyric poems: I couldn't soar over the hilly expanse of a good story, so I'd land here or there, wing-tired, and explore the moment, the detail. I was content to explore the side streets.

A decade ago I began to acknowledge a growing dissatisfaction with my poems. They looked smaller somehow, the ink on the page narrower. I repeated the word *spindly* over and over in my head while considering recent poems. *Stick legs* was another phrase that virtually announced itself as poems seemed to rise heroically from my page and… then quickly sit down again, winded, their skinny limbs barely up to the task of supporting their bodies. My poems began to resemble Giacometti's figures as stooped senior citizens, and as the work became

Joe Bonomo is the author of *AC/DC's Highway to Hell* (2010), *Jerry Lee Lewis: Lost and Found* (2009), *Installations* (2008), *Sweat: The Story of the Fleshtones, America's Garage Band* (2007), and numerous personal essays and prose poems. He teaches at Northern Illinois University.

physically undernourished, so did the subject matter. I was trying to translate the density of the moment—the side-glance of human mass that we're blessed with in ordinary domestic time—as a kind of prism through which many beams shine, but my poems were failing in their lean and dull ways. And what they had to say was becoming thin, mean, and, worse, esoteric, a kind of sterile cipher. Around this time my wife suggested that I write some prose.

I'd been mulling over a memory from school, an awful day when a bunch of my classmates threw stones at a girl named Mina because she was Iranian and Iran at that time held American hostages. In a brief prose piece I tried to write about the incident and whether or not I was implicated, worrying less about a beginning-middle-end than in circling the story though the indelible images I possessed of the day and era. I trusted that the common thread among them would be strong enough to bind together several pages, and it did. I began writing more essays, aligning myself with Montaigne's exercise of "essay" in *attempting* to make sense of the tones, sensations, and imagery my imagination clung to about occasions, trivial and large. I often had no idea where I'd land. More jagged than arced, these prose pieces began to coalesce into something more substantial, visually and thematically, than my poems. The magnetic right margin, with which I no longer danced self-consciously, tugged and lengthened my lines, layering them. And the discursive element and conversational voice relieved me (mostly) of the lyric, abstract tone with which my more recent poems had whispered, affectedly, to my ear.

My prose natively took shape as block text, but arranged musically, the sentences growing or shrinking organically. I approached the page with the same impulse I did when writing poetry: less with a subject than with a note struck inside of myself. And so my essays naturally hyphenate, sitting astride music and discourse, cadence and idea(s). I'll always lean toward the poetic with my feet firmly planted in the prosaic.

When I became interested in exploring nonautobiographical writing, I stuck with prose. I began to work on a biography of a cult rock & roll band, living and working in New York City for month-long stretches, poring over *Village Voice* microfilm in the New York Public Library, researching fabled neighborhoods and bars. As a (very) poor-man's Joe Mitchell, I was satisfying the urge to document an interesting era and world, but I felt the pull toward a more imaginative engagement. I'd become especially enamored with art installations, those lively, dimensional, arranged teasing of our environment. One of the last poems I'd written had described an early-1980s installation on the abandoned Lansburgh Building in old downtown Washington, D.C., where black cut-out figures had been mounted along the exterior ledges and windows, appearing to be scaling the building in a creepy-crawly manner. It had been an arresting and unnerving urban image.

When my attention turned to writing prose some years later, I revisited a poem that I'd written that had described a wholly fictional installation visited by a first-person persona; I relined the poem as prose, and was immediately struck. I created each installation fictionally, though many exhibited details borrowed from actual installations I'd read about or visited. Whatever "story" or "discourse" there might be in my description of any given installation was suggested and evoked by the arrangement of items. In essence, I was describing a poem with prose, was reporting on a visually poetic array, and the energy ignited between the lyrical and the reportage felt new, and very interesting— a compound of sorts. The prosody was pulling at the poetic to get into the game, to tell, to list, to name, to document, to report, to offer history, an artist's bio or manifesto; meanwhile the poetic was demurring, hoping that the prosiness would shut up for a second, be content to linger in the evoking of idea and concept by a still and quiet display of items and figures.

These installation prose poems began to tell a story. I imagined the same visitor at each installation, a curious museumgoer both eager and tentative, as each exhibit became weirder and stranger, luring him into a magic realist afternoon that accumulates as a story or a novel does. Encounters with other nameless visitors underscore the humane center of the installations, the pooling together in the wake of great art. Abandoning a conventional narrative arc, I simply dropped this guy into each room and watched the top of his head lift off. He'll leave that museum at the end of the day a very different man, the world having been re-presented to him in refreshing, startling ways.

Meanwhile I read, and reread: Baudelaire, Rimbaud, and Mallarmé, and Robert Bly, and I rediscovered Russell Edson. Edson's work has held up well since the 60s; his prose poems are smart and imaginative, the sur-realism and humor always finding firm footing in a recognizable world. Contemporary writers such as Tony Tost, Sarah Manguso, John D'Agata, and Joel Brouwer are producing vigorous, elastic prose poems as inter-esting intellectually as they are formally. Loitering happily at the prose/poetry intersection in journals such as *Quarter After Eight* and *Sentence*, I see that there are many writers who are naturally drawn there.

I'm attracted to writers extending the size and shape of the prose poem, often to book-length; if a prose poem extends to several pages or more, it can be read as a lyric essay: D'Agata in many of the *Halls of Fame* pieces, Brian Lennon throughout *City*. In this vein, D.J. Waldie and Robert Vivian are two writers who remain underappreciated. Waldie, in his brilliant *Holy Land: A Suburban Memoir*, creates a lyric map—if such a thing can be said to exist. Waldie's worked in a civic position in L.A. for decades, and his sometimes-fragmentary memories of growing up in mid-century suburban Los Angeles dovetail with accurate and clinical reportage of the area's tract history in 316 poetically arranged segments that suggest nothing less than an aerial view of a suburban neighbor-hood captured in reverie. A characteristic Vivian essay in *Cold Snap as Yearning* expounds upon a single image or a simple narrative moment, indulging in meditative vertical time as the rest of the world rushes for-ward, absorbed with itself. He seems nearly obsessed with Walter Pat-er's observation that all art "constantly aspires toward the condition of music," and with Mallarmé's notion that "the dream" of art is to suggest rather than to name. Vivian's lyric essays are less about anything solid, really, than about language and the imagination, and memory's stub-born insistence that both must give shape and substance to the world as perceived. These qualities give Vivian's best work a tenderness and sub-tlety, a prose-poem marriage of declaration and hush.

Although the prose poem has been with us for centuries, it feels new. There's something about our loud world, the daily collision of thought and noise, that's hospitable to the form. Postmodernism recognized cultural hybridization decades ago, and the further we are away from the formally tumultuous 70s and 80s, the era of collapsing definitions and crowded boundaries, the more clearly we see the inevitable ascension of a form that natively blends the lyric and the declarative. The line between the poetic and the statemental blurred as a consequence of the speed with which we live and perceive, inside of an era that welcomes and encourages The Hyphen. It's an obvious conclusion that this form will emerge as a major genre in this century.

POEMS

from Installations

A large, well-lit, white-walled room. You walk to a red line painted on the floor.

On the floor in front of you is a white-chalk outline of a body. You feel, *This is very much like a crime scene* and yet you don't shiver or look away.

There are several spectators with you. One walks to a low wood table near the red line and picks up a book. She leafs through. Over her shoulder you notice that the pages are empty.

She reads instructions printed on a placard nailed to the floor. She steps toward the chalk outline and kneels next to it. She opens the book she's holding to a random page of milk-white.

To your astonishment she stretches her body out and fits herself into the chalk outline. The outline matches her body perfectly, top-to-bottom, side-to-side.

She stands, walks over to you, and hands you the book. You confirm, leafing through the title, that the pages are blank. The cover is blank.

You step toward the chalk outline and, clutching the book awkwardly in one hand, sink to your knees, and then stretch your body inside the outline. To your astonishment the outline fits you perfectly. You feel transported, held, refreshed.

You stand up and hand the book to another spectator, who kneels at the outline, stretches his body, and lies in a flawless match.

You pick another book up from the low table. You wish that the book had words, you wish that you could read and understand. You wish that the book were titled *Empathy* in a language that you knew.

After Serving

I stuff my cassock in a closet. I dream of the Washington Redskins. I dream of Jenny and Wendy in pink underwear. I dream of an Italian sub. I dream of launching myself into the woods. I dream of bleeding sunlight. I dream of incense drifting into neglected corners. I dream of incense in haze. I dream loudly, as after silence. I dream of stink. I dream of counting sleepless heads in vapor. I dream of the change beneath my bed, and of transubstantiation. I dream of magic tricks evaporating, offered up into a noon sky. I dream of driving someday. I dream of the smell of ash wood, of the muddy field. I dream that the sun will continue its slow demise, someday giving up the far, pinched cry of the smothered baby. I dream of offering, of prayer, of social studies. I dream of the large, chapped fingers of the man whose hands I wash. I dream of the evacuated body. I dream of the altar. A sacristy is a room in a church. A cassock gropes emptily in a dark closet.

Gerry LaFemina

A CARNIVAL COMES TO TOWN
Showing Prose Poems at the County Fair

Around 1995 I was working with Sinan Toprak in translating the poems of Ali Yuce. Yuce is a contemporary Turkish poet; a socialist surrealist, his work was radically different from the meditative realism of my own lineated poems. For example, here is Yuce's "Feast":

Mama mouse sets the table
and then calls her spouse, the kids,
and her invited guests
who arrive gasping, excited
by the cat meat on the menu.

They ate, drank and burped.
They piled aboard a carriage made of an old trap
pulled by a noble tabby.
Inside, they carried on with gusto
riding to the festival.

If you win the race, said
Papa mouse to his boy,
I'll reward you with cat meat.
If you marry me, said
the girl mouse to her lover,
you'll never thirst for cat milk.[1]

Gerry LaFemina's latest book is the short story collection *Wish List* (2009). A new book of poems, *The Vanishing Horizon*, will be out in 2010 from Anhinga Press. His other books include the prose poetry collections *Zarathustra in Love* (2000) and *Figures from The Big Time Circus Book/The Book of Clown Baby* (2007). He directs the Frostburg Center for Creative Writing at Frostburg State University, where he also teaches.

After toiling on these translations, I'd return to my own work with a sense of confusion and anticipation. What should I do with this set of bizarre images that I'd collected in the meantime? Unable to return to my own aesthetic, I started to write in prose blocks—since the images themselves didn't seem to select a form for me, I wrote in what I then thought of as formlessness. The few contemporary American poems that resembled what I was doing were the prose poems of Michael Benedikt and Russell Edson; therefore, what I started writing when I returned to my own work became my first serious prose poems, prose poems that recognized genre.

Although there have been a number of pure prose poets recently, many contemporary poets have played with the writing of prose poems; the appeal of the form is simple enough: It seems limitless and full of limitations at the same time. It forces a writer to break his/her own rules, while adopting certain other criteria for judging the final product. Whereas in the contemporary free verse poem, formal inventiveness, careful use of lineation, and metrics help create tension, the prose poem is put in the rectangular light of its window: The sentence and the use of other poetic techniques (assonance, consonance, metaphor, alliteration) become all important. As does emphasis on image and lyricism. The lyric impulse is the heart of the best prose poems; this does not dismiss the need for or the urge for narrative—but purely narrative prose is not, by its very essence, prose *poetry*. It's important to note, too, that much of the criticism of the form stems from the very term "poetry" used in conjunction with "prose"—these detractors argue that lineation is the sole characteristic separating poetry from prose. Stephen Dunn called the pieces in his collection *Riffs & Reciprocities* (1998) paragraphs; David Ignatow complained "more than once ... that he felt his prose poetry had not been taken as seriously as his verse poetry."[2] David Lehman makes note of the fact that Mark Strand's *The Monument* (1978) was not awarded the Pulitzer Prize in 1978 because it was a col-

---

[1] Qtd. Yuce, Ali. "Feast." *Voice Lock Puppet.* Trans Sinan Toprak and Gerry LaFemina. Washington, DC: Orchises, 2002. 21

[2] Qtd. Johnson, Peter. "David Ignatow." *The Prose Poem: An International Journal* 7 (1998): 4.

lection of prose not poetry.[3] The prose poet, however, believes that lyricism and symbolism are more at the heart of poetry than lineation.

Liz Rosenberg says about the form "Its goal, simply put, is to let in more light. The view is wide. One tries, in the prose poem, to take in as much as possible. The prose poem generally lives in present tense."[4] The permanent present tense (the transcendent present tense) might just be an alternative definition for the lyric moment. But in the prose poem's fabulist tradition, the lyric bends the light in particular and surprising ways. In examples of the contemporary prose poem (I'm thinking of the work of Louis Jenkins and Cathryn Hankla), one sees an impulse toward lyricism first, toward imagism first, toward inventiveness first. Take, for example, "The Two Brothers" by Gian Lombardo:

> Surf revolves around them, a mile or so off-shore, as they rise out of the water to reach no great height. Their silence is broken only when it is night and they cannot be seen. Then the motions of the waves, white against brown by day, can be heard. Their sounds seem to form words that say, "I'll take no pity on those who cannot help being what they are," and then these sounds pull your sight from the North Star towards them, to undetermined chinks in the darkness. Water will pass as you strain to listen to them, from a fallow blue to crystal to faint clay sheen to a frozen grey. Overhead, a seagull cries.[5]

The narrative strain exists only as a device to promote and propel its lyric sensibility, emphasized by the aural image at the end.

In my own experience, I see the prose poem as a means to something lyrical that I can't *do* in other forms. They are uninvited guests who spice up the party. I like them—like writing them—because they are the place where the aesthetic censors I've set for myself are broken down. They are wormholes in the physics of my own writing universe. Whereas the

---

[3] Paraphrase. Lehman, David. "The Prose Poem: An Alternative to Verse." *APR* 32, 2 (2003): 45.

[4] Qtd. Rosenberg, Liz. "An Introductory Note to the Reader: Horizontal Windows." *These Happy Eyes*. DuBois, PA: Mammoth Books, 2001. 15.

[5] Qtd. Lombardo, Gian. "The Two Brothers." *Standing Room*. Baltimore, MD: Dolphin-Moon, 1989. 27.

poem for me starts with the line and its rhythm, the prose poem for me starts with the quirky and the sentence. If the lyric poem, for me, is a mirror to reality as I experience it, the prose poem holds up a fun house mirror to that reality.

If lyricism is the first tenant of prose poetry, there seems to be an essential and necessary element of surprise, of magic, of boundarylessness. The prose poem's very existence is an anomaly. Because it is both poem and prose, it, therefore, is neither poem nor prose. It's this neither/nor-ness that gives the form its startling energy, that says to the writer: *I dare you*... It is this nature that gives the writer freedom to make astonishing leaps, where the poet finds the energy of myth. It is the doorway at the very beginning of each episode of *The Twilight Zone*: It leads to another dimension. Charles Simic defines the form as "the culinary equivalent of peasant dishes, like paella or gumbo, which bring together a great variety of ingredients or flavors, and which in the end, thanks to the art of the cook, somehow blend. Except, the parallel is not exact. Prose poetry does not follow a recipe. The dishes it concocts are unpredictable and often vary from poem to poem."[6]

This is true primarily because it is not anything particular, and therefore the prose poem, for all its boxiness, can be anything. Think of the rectangles in your life: The midway booth where you shoot water into clown mouths, the bed you dream in, the gift-wrapped box. Louis Jenkins says about the shape: "The box is made for travel, quick and light. … One must pack carefully, only the essentials, too much and the reader won't get off the ground. Too much and the poem becomes a story, a novel, an essay or worse…. The trick to writing a prose poem is discovering how much is enough and how much is too much. It's a matter of maintaining balance."[7]

Consider the prose poem a magic box, similar to the one magicians use to make things appear or disappear. In "Ars (Prose) Poetica" I write:

---

[6] Qtd. Simic, Charles. "A Long Course in Miracles." *Pretty Happy* by Peter Johnson. Fredonia, NY: White Pine Press, 1997. 16.

[7] Qtd. Jenkins, Louis. "A Few Words about the Prose Poem." *Nice Fish: New and Selected Prose Poems*. Duluth, MN: Holy Cow!, 1995.

And the thing is you could put anything in it—a loop of Rosary beads, old love letters, a favorite pair of shoes. Close the box. Turn it once, twice, thrice, and say some magic nonsense, whatever words flutter in your mouth. If you do it right, if you turn the box correctly, if you practiced hard enough, the contents will be gone. In their place: a snow ball, the stems of wildflowers, a goldfish swimming in a favorite tea cup.

Of course, the words aren't nonsense—but the point about practice is true. As is a willingness to conduct magic. If one approaches the form in this manner, then one can achieve what David Young refers to as "the essential craziness and exuberant inventiveness that we take to be the especially representative flavor of the genre."[8]

The prose poem then is more than just a poem without line breaks, but a demanding form unto itself. Free verse poets often claim that they have to be more vigilant in their work than formalists because they're the makers of the rhythm, the line breaks have to be determined, etc; prose poems require a different kind of vigilance than free verse poetics, and their essential material may be very different. In my own work, the driving force in a new poem is linear, a rhythmic unit that gathers emotional and lyric momentum as I pursue it, as I discover what material it will untangle. In my prose poems it's an image, a sensibility, the beginning of myth that leads me to discovery. In *Zarathustra in Love* (2000), I have several pieces that began as "failed" poems because the sensibility of the given work did not lend itself to lineation. Converted to prose poems in revision, the pieces sprang to life, as if finally planted in the right soil.

I came to the prose poem as someone looking for something to do with these raffish images, the surprising and shocking ones that were released via my translation project. What happened when I started to write them, however, was a real connection to many things I felt never fit into my poems: Bigfoot, late night television, four years of a philosophy major, a love for circuses, and a video library full of old chillers; I

[8] Qtd. Young, David. "Introduction." *Models of the Universe: An Anthology of the Prose Poem.* Eds. David Young and Stuart Friebert. Oberlin, OH: Oberlin College Press, 1995. 19.

also could include a number of things that do fit into my poems—such as an emotional and spiritual inquisitiveness. For me, prose poems are like the line of trucks and vans that bring the carnival to town: Filled with folded-down rides, games of chance, fun house mirrors, cotton candy and carnies themselves who are both kind of scary and kind of intriguing. They carry with them the ability to bring immense joy in very basic and surprising ways.

When I go into the writing of a new prose poem I have no clue what the fairground will hold, what surprise I may find. I just know that anything is possible, that the mythic and the banal can be holding hands on the Ferris wheel, and that, if the moon is right, they just might kiss. The prose poem has no concern with a story that starts at home with "characters" trying to decide whether we should go to the carnival; the prose poem has no reason to capture all that narrative, but it should capture the moonlight, and the lips, the spin of that Ferris wheel, and the way one looks at oneself afterward in the fun house mirrors, alone and misshapen.

POEMS

Existentialism

When you're in a bar you can be anything, so says my father-in-law. Today is Gordie Howe's birthday, and he and Gordie are about the same age, so maybe tonight, at this tavern, he could be Gordie Howe, but we're outside Detroit where everyone knows Gordie Howe—Mr. Hockey they call him. People see him in a bar they say, *Hey Mr. Hockey*!

No one ever says that to my father-in-law.

Still, I know what he means. When I was a bouncer, I'd see how a few rounds could transform four college guys into the young philosophers guild, a bunch of Descartes-wannabes, drinking and therefore being. O! How the hours passed as they deconstructed a beer label, argued the phenomenology of a juke box, developed a metaphysics of getting rejected by women. As I walked the crowd, always some-one different, I listened to them tell their impossible lies, beginning with their names, and encompassing the entire stories of their ordinary lives.

Pancake House Is Made of Pancakes

–headline from the Weekly World News
– for Lori Yoder

Pancake house is made of pancakes. Treehouse is made of trees. Townhouse is made of towns: Frostburg, which is frigid; Friendsville, where everyone knows your name, is neighborly, hugs you when you leave; Mechanicsburg, where everybody owns a tool-set, gets greasy in their garages; Laboratory (Pennsylvania), where the houses are all test tubes, each family an experiment; Eighty-four (also Pennsylvania), that town of octogenarians. Of course, the greenhouse is made of greens—100 shades, and its lawn is a putting green. Animal house is made of animals. Ditto doghouse, specifically dogs. And the birdhouse is made of birds, though right now the walls have flown off—a flock of gulls and sparrows. See how they're gorging themselves right now on the roof of our pancake house.

Ray Gonzalez

NO TONGUE IN CHEEK
The True Frame of the Prose Poem

When I write prose poems, the main truth I confront is the fact that the paragraph I am trying to bring to life is a poetic form in itself, though one that gives me an odd freedom to write away from lyrical stanzas, line breaks, and the isolation of individual words. This kind of truth magnetizes form and subject, until the prose poem forces me to be honest toward its composition into one or more paragraphs. This honesty means each prose poem I write has to sustain its form through the cluster of sentences it is allowing. When the sentences work in grammatical and lyrical methods, the factor of surprise is heightened. Truth in prose poetry forces me to maintain the paragraph in a poetic atmosphere, while I attempt to break out of its boundaries. This is done through a language that speaks both within and outside the block form.

Zbigniew Herbert, the great Polish poet, approaches truth in his prose poem, "Wall." While the content and lyricism can be found in a poem built in stanzas, this block form allows the poet's higher measures of eternity to rise above the sentences:

Wall

We stand against the wall. Our youth has been taken from us like a condemned man's shirt. We wait. Before the fat bullet lodges itself

Ray Gonzalez is the author of 17 books of poetry, fiction, and nonfiction and the editor of 12 anthologies. His most recent books include *Cool Auditor: Prose Poems* (2009), *Faith Run: Stanza Poems* (2009), and a collection of essays, *Renaming the Earth* (2008). He is co-editor, with Robert Shapard and James Thomas, of *Sudden Fiction Latino: Short Short Stories from the U.S. and Latin America* (2010). He is the director of the MFA Program in Creative Writing at the University of Minnesota in Minneapolis.

in our necks, ten or twenty years pass. The wall is high and strong. Behind the wall there are a tree and a star. The tree is lifting the wall with its roots. The star is nibbling the stone like a mouse. In a hundred, two hundred years there will be a little window.

To look beyond the lines that form the wall and allow the creation of the window is the approach of a truth that applies to any prose poem of integrity. Herbert opens the world of war and tragedy by compressing time and its moments of revelation. In a way, the poem reads like a note, a reminder to the reader and the eternal survivor that there may be a way into the poem and an exit toward life. This journey is through the window of time, revelation, and human understanding. Again, these are universal truths one can find in traditional poetic forms, yet what Herbert accomplishes on a higher level is pushed into the paragraph function of the prose poem because the paragraph is a timeless concept that reinforces truth-telling by the way it uses words whose visual and linear characteristics are not bound by set patterns. Yes, the paragraph is a pattern, but its words within are constantly moving across a kaleidoscope that enlarges the poem.

Herbert's influence on my own prose poems is hard to measure, not because it is transparent or subjective, but because the prose poetry of "little windows" contains a poetic power that allows true strains of the self to be woven into a text that stands on its own, carries the measure of influence, and composes a fresh stage. In other words, a prose poem written in response to great prose poets like Herbert, Charles Baudelaire, Russell Edson, or Charles Simic is the kind of paragraph that announces it is constructed out of a truth-telling that bridges the elements of poetry and nonfiction. And, in the case of prose poetry, the element of nonfiction applies to real details, setting, and even the psychic make-up of the poet. The lyrical or poetic strain comes through the imagination, the influence, and responses to the world through the multi-layered plains of language. It is not an ideal marriage because Herbert's little window is constantly tempted to close, completely shutting off the poet from his material. This is where the freedom of the prose poem comes into the picture—the prose poet does not allow the text to fail or remain incomplete because the uncanny form of a poem-in-paragraph propels the writer beyond the trappings of a lyrical tradition that often make the poet stop writing. The window stays wide open and the truth of the poem emerges because a poem as paragraph is a living text without boundaries placed on thought and meaning.

My prose poem "Sticky Monkey Flowers, Monterey Bay" is not about the violence between men and their centuries, as the Herbert poem, though it was influenced by "Wall" in the way it looks beyond the obvious and attempts to find a way out of vision—a way of seeing that focuses on the present moment, even as the poet acknowledges what has come before is never going to alight itself right in front of his eyes:

Sticky Monkey Flowers, Monterey Bay

Blossoms scrambled in the eye of tomorrow, bright little fires outlining the shape of secrecy, actual light of measure wounded by consequence, given color against argument, in favor of remorse as the flower is handled without letting go of its green veins—fragile lines toward the surf hitting shore as if something was thrown out there long ago. When flight kept track of that line of pelicans, there was a roar across the bay, distant white specks in the sky vanishing like the seeds of this nourishment, their cold pardons a combination of infinite movement and the words for the kindest news. Sticky monkey flowers spreading into sunlit nerves, moving in the mist like a distant yellow horizon taking its time coming back. Blossoms lifting, small and untroubled, given their green moisture to fill the eye after the fever breaks, after sands drift into hidden coves of disaster, one lone pelican making it back in time to avoid the shape moving across the plants that twist sand with wind, flower scent with muscle, leaving the unknown out of the garden, the unspoken out of the rising drifts of what has been.

My complete truths are hidden in the poem and its block density invites the readers' interpretations because its character attracts such dissection. My reality is revealed through the details that a piece of nonfiction commonly builds upon. This is a prose poem because I am showing what I see and I am inside the poem and outside of it. It is nonfiction, and some readers argue that many prose poems are miniature essays because any kind of movement through the text is completely on the level surface of experience and understanding, despite certain unrevealed mysteries that could take the piece in other directions. This is what a prose poem does—joins the poetic shadows of deception and clarity with the sunlit, open windows of a nonfictional confrontation with what lies in front of the writer for any reader to see. At this point, I must repeat myself and demand that attention be paid to the fact, once again, that these things are being done in sentences and paragraphs and the prose poet has said farewell to the line break and stanza in the same manner that Herbert's wall is lifted by the roots of the tree.

The immense waters that line the horizon of Monterey Bay blink toward a distant line of pelicans as they approach the beach. I stand in clusters of sticky monkey flowers and smell the fresh oblivion of a distance only a poet can imagine, capture, and realign on the page. These acts naturally condense into paragraph form because what I see across the bay and the affirming approach of the huge, white birds creates questions whose answers have woven a prose response even before I know I am going to react in that style. The prose poem is suited for this experience because the visual aspects of what I see are layers of perception, emotion, and detailed awareness whose weight collapses in early attempts at the traditional poem. They fall into themselves, perhaps having entered through the little window I have been given because the poet standing alone on the beach gathers the immensity of their being and recreates how they fall upon each other in a coagulating syntax that wants nothing to do with the same, old poetic patterns.

This means the prose poem evolved before its author even realized it. This flavor of truth, and the idea that poetry is already there and the poet goes to it, is not mysterious or has anything to do with a sense of the Muse. The prearranged prose poem, moving in my direction in the shape of the immense Monterey waters and the captivating pelicans, comes into my awareness only after I step out of the sticky monkey flowers to thwart the impulse toward stanzas. The truth of the prose poem is given, not felt. The actuality of a linear, lined poem is felt and not given. The Monterey Bay experience is given to me in a very honest manner because the prose telling, the prose journey, and the prose magnet of words were already there, waiting to be identified by standing on the beach and contemplating the world. These conclusions often cause some of the sharpest debates over the prose poem. I pronounce them because the window of accepting my experience at Monterey and being able to write about it in a truthful manner hung over the salty waters until I went and plucked them in the same awkward manner some of those pelicans picked fish out of the water. The "actual light of manner wounded in consequence" I recognize along the shore is a moment when I admit I cannot lie about what I see or what the shoreline makes me ponder. It is a complex recognition that arrives in a paragraph that stays with me before I set it down on paper. When I write the words, "Blossoms lifting, small and untroubled, given their green moisture to fill the eye after the fever breaks," I allow these temperatures of knowing and trust to pattern themselves into sentences that are "leaving the unknown out of the garden, the unspoken out of the rising drifts of what has been." My prose poem has done this because what it contains is exactly what I want to say and I will not hide behind vague poetic dimensions to say it. The block of words does not allow me to hide behind grammatical curtains.

One of the most important sentences in Herbert's "Wall" is "The star is nibbling the stone like a mouse." It is crucial in understanding truth in a prose poem because this demand for existence and knowledge cannot be measured through the immensity of established patterns of poetic discourse. The star will completely absorb the stone in the same manner my blossoms lift, small and untroubled, after the fever of experience has ended. They rise out of the paragraph and give off their powerful scent because I have confessed. As I finish writing the prose poem, this confession burns with a temperature that cannot be measured because a line, then a sentence, and finally—a paragraph have been identified in the shape of a prose poem whose window is unlocked and about to be shattered.

POEMS

As We Get Closer to the Apricot

As we get closer to the apricot, there is a reward between the sunflowers and the last place we stood when we were young, this revelation delivered by two fighting sparrows twisting in circles under the bird feeder, their encounter interrupted by the white squirrel leaping at the pole holding the feeder. It drives the birds away, its white tail brushing the air like the last letter from the alphabet needed to complete the sentence that gets closer to the apricot sitting in a blue bowl on the kitchen table, its bruise changing shape within its hairy skin to align itself with the sunlight coming through the window.

The Spine

The step I take lives besides the indefinite aspect of a universal tool melting toward a crown of thorns embedded in the spine of principle, its forehead playing paradise with the brain. The frame I border with flowered articulation involves roots and branches spreading into a form of disdain, cancelled moments where the spine touches an equal measure of mouth.

The arm I move with invented awareness folds into impossible strength, its velocity tracing microscopic paths upon the mole on my leg, its eye abandoned by the resting spine. The faithful gesture, articulating loss and theft, insists on engines developing a method for extracting the spine from my thirst, replanting it beyond convictions I haven't explained.

The likeness I position between the storm and my hands is also placed at the table where the spine sits to judge my need to get out of the way when it stands up on its own and I stare at what looks like a bone-white man—no arms, no legs, simply the spine of where he originates.

Maureen Seaton

MOVING VIOLATIONS
The Prose Poem as Fast Car

When I matured as a poet, I serendipitously (and surreptitiously) matured into the prose poem. (Had I wearied of the line break in much the same way as I'd wearied of polyester? Catholicism?) It was an unplanned homecoming for me, and it seemed risky, more a coming out than a coming home. My computer simply lost control, throwing longer and longer lines without thought of organization until I wondered if I had the right to call what I was messily creating *poetry*.

I'd read Rimbaud, Baudelaire, Gertrude Stein, Russell Edson, Maxine Chernoff: respected predecessors all. In the early 90s, whenever I taught the prose poem, I patterned exercises after them so my students could experience undergrad irony and we could laugh at the geniuses among us.

But many of my own prose poems weren't so funny. I involuntarily used the small rectangle as a bomb. Or an urn. I taught Joy Harjo's *In Mad Love and War* and Alicia Ostriker's "Cambodia." There was that implicit irony, but it was of the pissed off variety—or else a cap on grief. At times I seemed to be writing from within the (four) walls of the poem, pushing against prescription. "It doesn't take a visionary to see the box," says poet and critic Holly Iglesias, "just experience inside one." As Iglesias, in her book *Boxing inside the Box: Women's Prose Poetry*, suggests of other women poets, from Sei Shōnagon to Kimiko Hahn and Carolyn Forché,

Maureen Seaton's publications include *Cave of the Yellow Volkswagen* (2009); *Sex Talks to Girls: A Memoir* (2008), winner of the Lambda Literary Award; *Venus Examines Her Breast* (2004), winner of the Audre Lorde Award; and *Furious Cooking* (1996), winner of the Iowa Poetry Prize and the Lambda Literary Award. The recipient of an NEA Fellowship and a Pushcart Prize, Seaton teaches poetry at the University of Miami.

I used the prose poem as "pressure cooker, sand box, sanctuary, laboratory, dungeon, treasure chest." In that contained space, I discovered, embraced, and wrestled worlds.

Some of my prose poems felt fast, like strapping myself into a roller coaster and riding it all the way down, left to right, top to bottom, until the wild mouse crashed into the final image. Or like driving my imaginary friend, my Nissan Skyline GT-R, on Route 40 through New Mexico. I loved the way that felt. Opening a vein. Baffling the radar. I also loved stopping (like at the top of a Ferris wheel), taking a breath while balancing mid-air, then off I'd go again: poems with several prose stanzas, boxes on boxes filled with jetsam and doubloons.

I'd found *Praise*. It was the first time I consciously experienced another poet—Robert Hass—playing with breath by using line breaks *and* prose. I didn't set out to imitate, but I'm thinking my computer might have. I loved mixing, layering, collaging. My computer knew how to do these things easily. In *Praise*, "The Beginning of September" and "The Yellow Bicycle," both of which alternate prose and verse stanzas, enthralled and fed me. They still do. They shake it up for me. That doesn't mean I didn't memorize "Meditation at Lagunitas" and "The Garden of Delight" (both superbly line-broken) so I'd have something to summon up if I were ever incarcerated or marooned. But when it came to the writing itself, I'd crossed over from what I now call single-surfaced to layered poems (although there are a million ways besides structurally to layer)—and, except for terza rima, which is like a beloved tic for me, I have only rarely gone back to traditional forms or free verse.

I recently overheard a critic say that some poems are more fun to write than to read. I was extremely sensitive to this possibility when these new babies started flying out of me. They thwarted the expectations, I believed then, of most of the folks who would ever want to pick up a book of poems. Poem lovers expect air on the page, I thought, gulps of negative space after lines, between stanzas, allowing for breath, enjambment, more breath, creating music, which, everyone knows, is a key element in the art of poetry. And there I was, creating claustrophobia and apparently no music at all—perhaps just noise—without any regard for the reader. I was embarrassed because my prose poems were dense and long, and I was more embarrassed thinking about the people I loved who would feel even farther away from my poet self now that I was offering them ungainly chunks of text to ponder.

"Which would you prefer to read?" I said, presenting my daughters with two specimens—one in prose and one with line breaks. "This," said the daughter who likes to read poetry, pointing to the page with fresh air built in. "This," said the other, who normally prefers to read fiction, pointing to the choking text. "But I'm not so sure I'd call it a poem, Mom."

Was I really a poet? Didn't I know that the very act of breaking the line—the execution of the line, not the sentence—was sacrosanct? Maybe I was a writer of tiny fictions or tiny memoirs or, as a Miami student of mine said recently, "stubby creatures" (thanks, Rafael). This was all happening in 1994, which is when I got my first laptop. I hadn't heard of flash fiction yet. And when I did, I knew it wasn't what I was doing. But how did I know that?

I once came up with a way to teach my Chicago student poets the (un)canny "difference" between the prose poem and poetic prose, which may also be slantily translated into the "PP or FF" (prose poem/flash fiction) debate of recent years. This genre business has often baffled my students, and my answer of "The writer gets to say" has appealed to very few of them. "The reader gets to say" appeals even less. My metaphor may work only in Chicago, but here it is.

Late November and early April often look the same in the city of Chicago. If you've got a yard (and many people do), you might notice that everything seems dead out there during both of those times. No green anywhere, just gray and brown and bleak. Yet one month is the beginning of winter and one is the end. So how would you know if it's fall or spring? Well, you wouldn't, at least not by looking, my students admitted. But it is, nevertheless, one season or the other, I'd say, waiting for a possible light to go on about what essentializes prose and poetry. I always worry that I'm too laissez-faire for most of my students; but, really, what I myself think: Who cares what season it is—just write!

I once unconsciously chose and now consciously choose process over product or artifice. For me, the prose poem provides the perfect container—like any favorite form might—and then it dispenses with the container as well. I spend precious time fitting the text I've streamed to the music I hear. It's still metered, but it's internal. I hear sounds for particular words too, that's why streaming works well for me—the poem feeds me the sound and sometimes I get it right the first time and sometimes I have to think about the sound and then the sense that's bubbling up and find the sound—like the way the person typing subtitles on live TV goes back and retypes a word or phrase when the meaning catches up. That's how prose poems come to me, the sound of the words arriving first, no interruptions, no restraints, the rhythm kicking in—my twin turbo six-cylinder cutting through wind—all horizon and velocity.

POEMS

The Realm of the Wide

(i)

Every time I land a word, it loses cells and runs a temperature. You could jump the fire and ride to where the words are backdrafting. Feel yourself mingle with the word you love beside you. The way it moves, a delicate fish, a purple cut-out of a delicate fish, a shadow of a cut-out of a fish, salty sex.

The word: Outlandish.

She stands on the cliff and her head whirs like a halo, a terrible needle, the spin of a bird in the bush, extravagant as a newborn, expensive as the fare to far-off places like Hempstead, New York.

Firefighter, cop, Trojan horse. The elevator climbs to the top of the Sears Tower in three minutes flat although no one counts or maybe a certain person whose mind is always ticking might count, a person in love with beats or time. If everything could be a brief slice of bluefish on a plate. But this moon has got me up the way someone comes in and drags you out of bed to play cards or eat mayonnaise on toast at 3 am or dance with her dance with her.

(ii)

- baby pigs
- distracted father
- long bungee cord attached to car
- clown nose and glasses
- a shaman in a wheelchair

There were baby pigs of all sizes from a couple of inches to a few pounds feeding on piles of scraps. Dad drove a long car with a bungee cord attached to the back in order to extricate his children from some (or the) danger. However, when it was my turn, he forgot I was there and started driving very fast around impossible suburbs. Then there was the old married couple who reminded me of the couple in *The Reluctant Shaman*. He was in a wheelchair and handed me his clown nose and glasses and then it was my turn to sit in the wheelchair and wear the clown nose and glasses. I can't remember if people could tell us apart or not. It mattered, but only slightly.

(iii)

Sorrowful _____

Joyful _____

Glorious _____.

Roll the mysteries around like hard candy, slang and tangle, peak and slide—the spontaneous combustion of the orange of the words, the crunch and smack, fossil and pictograph, a whole dam of rocks, stones, and words.

(iv)

Many travelers choose to make a voyage to the Blessed Realms of the West in a small boat, there to encounter many tests, challenges and changes. They often take these voyages seemingly by accident; they become exiled from their own land, and enter the realm of the wide and trackless sea. (The heated stones themselves go into and come out of the water.)

(v)

She chopped all the heads off Mary in Joliet then came to Chicago to study art. It was like this before I met her, the baseball bats, the small heads rolling across lawns and mangers. Mâché brains scattered like seed, that smirk of conception, that maculate homespun Mom.

"People who look for symbolic meanings fail to grasp the inherent mystery of the image. No doubt they sense this mystery, but they wish to get rid of it." —René Magritte

"Vanilla is the purest form of truth." —Nick

Ice

We were driving down the Kennedy having a great time guessing old groups Spinners Commodores La Belle maybe I was driving fast we'd been cold for a month not regular cold scary the kind that wears you down twenty forty below dark so cold you know hell is scratchy wool and miles of hard ice forget heat and everything suddenly stopped the Lincoln which was not our Lincoln but my sister's boyfriend's Lincoln not even his but the leased whim of a fired employee crashed into the back of a steel-gray Mercedes Benz you could feel the ice eat your bones your bumpers the plastic grill curling up the back of the Mercedes Jesus that Lincoln imploded good old American the Mercedes owner said as we shook in the ridiculous cold cars whizzing down the frozen highway and Lori's arm shot across my chest like a mother's we'd been spoons sleeping on the sunny couch earlier while the temperature reached a record low in Chicago my ex-husband used to say stop breathing on my back Maureen the only thing I remember about the crash is the way Lori's left arm reached out and saved me from ice crystals on the windshield she said whenever I breathe on her back she melts.

John Bradley

WHATCHAMACALLIT & ME

If you want to understand the prose poem, someone once told me, you should read Charles Baudelaire's *Paris Spleen*. And so I did. After reading those deliciously malevolent whatchamacallits, I came away thinking— Ah, so this is what decadent French writers, who have a love/hate relationship with Paris, write. Now I realize I was wrong. It's what decadent American writers, with a love/hate relationship with pretty much everything, write.

~

I call the prose poem the whatchamacallit, as most of us, prose poem practitioners included, cannot define it. I've been to prose poem panel after befuddled panel at writing conferences where whirling panelists chase their tails trying to define the whatchamacallit. I've tail-chased too. Michael Benedikt, in his long out-of-print *The Prose Poem: An International Anthology*, bravely offers this definition: "A genre of poetry, self-consciously written in prose, and characterized by the intense use of devices of verse." I would have to amend this, though, so it would read, "often unself-consciously." At least for me.

~

This Is Not a Prose Poem (Probably)

"Arguments continue about whether prose poetry is actually a form of poetry or a form of prose (or a separate genre altogether). Most critics

John Bradley is the author of three prose poetry collections: *Add Musk Here* (2002), *War on Words* (2006), and *You Don't Know What You Don't Know* (forthcoming). His prose poetry can also be found in *The Best of the Prose Poem* and *No Boundaries*. He is the recipient of a Pushcart Prize and two NEA Fellowships for poetry and teaches at Northern Illinois University.

argue that prose poetry belongs in the genre of poetry because of met-aphorical language and attention to language. Other critics argue that prose poetry falls into the genre of prose because prose poetry relies on prose's association with narrative, its consistent divergence of discourse, and its reliance on readers' expectations of an objective presentation of truth in prose. Yet others argue that the prose poem gains its subversive-ness through its fusion of both poetic and prosaic elements."
—Your Pretty Smart Friends @ Wikipedia.com

~

I can't remember writing my first prose poem. I do remember from time to time making these small bricks of prose when trying to distill a haunt-ing dream. If I tried to do this in verse, the distillation process lost much of the essence of the dream. By omitting odd details—the small white papery circles on my wife's winter coat, for example—in an attempt to make the poem attain a larger significance, the uniqueness and strange-ness of the dream utterly vanished. But the prose poem could retain, or perhaps recreate, the dream world.

Soon I had a handful of these little whatchamacallits, and so when a notice appeared one day in *Poets & Writers* calling for submissions for the first issue of Peter Johnson's *The Prose Poem: An International Jour-nal*, I sent them off. Finally, a zoo for whatchamacallits.

(Thank you, Peter. I think.)

~

I devoured Robert Bly's *Morning Glory* when it first came out, amazed at how these prose poems could both vividly describe the mundane and wildly associate from those objects (racing stripes on a turtle!). I knew, however, that my prose poems were doing something different. They shared a kinship with the short prose of Franz Kafka, Julio Cortázar, as well as with the paintings of Hieronymus Bosch and Frida Kahlo. Not to mention TV dinners.

For me, the prose poem offers a pathway into the subconscious, with its unexpected quick cast, costume, and landscape changes. With its startling juxtapositions, irrational situations, and dark humor. With its encounters with the everyday and the inexplicable—where these often intertwine. Verse keeps trying to shed the unpoetic detail (the girl who

I ran over in one dream, who had a piece of masking tape on her chest with the name SPUD written on it—how could I ever get her in verse?), while the prose poem thrives on specificity and the tangential (or what appears tangential). For me, the verse poem employs a fastidious bouncer, choosey about who will be allowed in, while the prose poem is a shark. It swallows everything. Including, at times, me.

~

One of my favorite prose poems is Guillermo Samperio's "Free Time" (translated by Russell M. Cluff and L. Howard Quackenbush, in *New Writing from Mexico*, a special issue of *TriQuarterly*). Like Franz Kafka's "Metamorphosis," it's a story of transformation, only here, instead of beginning with a transformation (Gregor Samsa waking as a whatchamacallit) we watch the transformation slowly take place. On what seems like an ordinary morning, our unnamed narrator buys the morning paper and ink smears on his hand. But the ink won't come off. Annoyed, the narrator calls the newspaper to complain: "While I was talking on the phone, I realized it wasn't a stain at all, but rather an infinite number of tiny letters tightly packed together, like a swarming multitude of black ants." Soon the narrator becomes a newspaper, which his wife calmly picks up and begins to read.

I've read this prose poem many times, and each time I'm captivated by it. In less than a page, we've taken a journey, one that leaves us unsure about reality. It's as if we're listening to a friend telling us how she got sick last week, starting with the first symptoms. We wonder about our own vulnerability. This newspaper transformation syndrome could be viral; we're all susceptible.

~

Other favorite prose poems: Robert Bly's "The Dead Seal," Carolyn Forché's "The Colonel," Robert Hass' "A Story about the Body," Franz Kafka's "Leopards in the Temple," Jamaica Kincaid's "Girl," Francis Ponge's "The Pleasures of the Door," and Russell Edson's "A Performance at Hog Theater" (though my list of Edson favorites could go on for pages).

Some favorite books of prose poems: Nin Andrews' *The Book of Orgasms*, Eric Baus' *The To Sound*, Jenny Boully's *The Body*, Lyn Hejinian's *My Life*, Louis Jenkins' *An Almost Human Gesture*, George Kalamaras' *Even the Java Sparrows Call Your Hair*, Daniil Kharms' *Today I Wrote Nothing*, Lautréamont's *Maldoror*. And every book of Russell Edson's.

~

Edson makes it look so easy: "A man straddling the apex of his roof cries, giddyup," or "There was once a hog theater where hogs performed as men, had men been hogs," or "Cows they had, many, drifting like heavy clouds in the meadow." With a deadpan rivaling Buster Keaton's, he makes me laugh, yet while I'm laughing, I know there's much more going on than the humor of a great standup-prose-poem comedian. He's subversive, with an air of nonchalance about his subversiveness: "In spite even of Columbus the world collapses and goes flat again." In Edsonland, the world as we know it is subject to whims, fears, and delights. Reason becomes an itch that the imagination will scratch. Edson's been doing this since the early 60s, and he's maintained the same style, voice, tone, though literary movements and styles have crashed upon the shores and receded many times since then.

~

One of the problems with writing prose poems is that now every poem I start to write has to be tested; does it want to be verse, or a prose poem? I often find myself trying out two versions of the same piece, one in verse and one in prose. I set the two versions aside and come back later to decide. Usually when I come back weeks or months later I can tell—or think I can.

I was working on something called "The Vomit Tax" recently, inspired by a news story about a tax on college students who, after a night of drinking, vomit in their dorms. They must pay a tax for the privilege of dorm vomiting. Then, hope the administrators, students might not drink as much, or barf in the bushes, or out the dorm window.

At first, I tried a verse poem. Surely a discussion of vomit taxation would be even more comical if conducted with shapely verse lines, I thought. But when I came back recently to reread the poem, I knew I was wrong. It had to be a prose poem, safe house for the lost, absurd, and scarily humorous.

~

The Story of X: This Is Not a Prose Poem (Probably)

X, a verse poet who defected to the dark side of prose poetry, tells me he applied several times for a state arts council grant. Each time he had no luck. Could it be because X kept sending them prose poems? Surely no one would be discriminating against prose poems, he thought, not after the way the prose poem has been recognized as a legitimate art form. Still, he wondered.

So one year X did a sneaky thing. He took the prose poems he had been sending to the arts council, and broke them into verse. Silly, he thought, but still, what if? he wondered.

That year X's state arts council gave him a grant for poetry.

~

Though there are still pockets of resistance to the prose poem, it continues to gain widespread acceptance. Can anyone keep track of all the prose poem collections that come out each year? And because the whatchamacallit gains literary acceptance, there will be a backlash. My crystal ball tells me that prose poets will be hunted down, subjected to special interrogation methods, tried by a military tribunal, and sentenced to write sonnets, and nothing but sonnets. I see the accused tossed in the air, and if they fly, they will have proven they are not prose poets. I could be mistaken, however, as my crystal ball tells me Dick Cheney is a closet prose poet. Hence the body-sized safe in his bunker, full of whatchamacallits.

~

"We live by tunneling for we are people buried alive," Anne Carson tells us, in her prose poem "On Orchids." If she's right, and we are "buried alive," with language, images, ads, advice, warnings, etc., the prose poem mirrors this state of being. It presents the eye with the visual equivalent of being buried in layers of stuff. And yet, at the same time, it offers a way out—those slim tunnels between the relentless lines of babble. Not bad for a mere whatchamacallit.

~

How many prose poets does it take to change a lightbulb?
Ask me later. We're still debating the question, "What is a lightbulb?"

POEMS

I Shall Be Released

I once dated a woman who had a minuscule role (she bit the head off a marigold) in a movie that was never released but gained cult status mostly because it was never released. "Doesn't faze me," she'd tell me, but I wondered why she used the word "released" for making love, as in, "Let's get released," instead of "Let's make Milwaukee moan," or "Let's boil the carpet," or "Let's cremate the goldfish."

Whenever I took a photo of her, she pulled a strand of hair over one eye, or shook her head so hair covered her face, or stood so that you could only see her staring back at you through one eye. "Is Rene feeling all right?" my mother asks me in the kitchen. "She seems a little, you know." "She's fine, really, mom," I tell her. "She's just waiting to be released."

Rolling down the driveway, thinking about the taste of marigolds, I command my right foot to stomp upon the brake, but my foot says, "Commander, that order is not a feasible option at this particular moment in perpetual time," so the unslowed car plows into the neighbor's organic kabuki garden. For this I must admit I gained a certain level of renown on that street and several interconnected streets adjacent thereto.

Parable of the Astral Wheel

"I wonder where your brother is," my father says, puffing on his briar pipe at the train station, gazing up at the portly pigeons in the rafters. The station has been closed for decades, but I don't tell him. "Should have been here hours ago," he notes. I ask if I can polish his shoes. I open the wooden barrel that serves as my stool and storage unit, find the ox blood polish, open the can and spit into the polish as he taught me to do when I was a child. He pretends to read *Time* magazine, but I know he's studying my every move. When I'm done buffing his shoes to an obnoxious shine, I sit back and wait. He glances down at his shoes and says, "Just a little more spit."

I ask him if he'd like a pack of gum, a comb, condoms, a radioactive tumbleweed, an astral prayer. "I wonder," he says, "what's keeping your brother." I don't tell him that my brother left us years ago. "He never would have left, you know, if I had read the Bible every day," he tells me. "You'll like the astral prayer," I tell him. "It's completely silent and no one can see it, and your every movement spins out a prayer." He sadly shakes his head. "If only we had listened to the priest," he says, "and when he was a baby had his little butt sewn shut."

Nin Andrews

MY NUDE EMPRESS

I always love to do things the wrong way. Wear the wrong clothes, say the wrong things, think the wrong thoughts. I like a certain degree of mess, chaos, mystery, randomness. I don't want things that are too polished, too clean, too "done." Like perfectly coiffed men or women without a single hair out of place. They give me hives.

By definition, and even by nature, I think a poet is someone obsessed with order. Someone who can't stop rhyming, repeating, primping, or fixing herself up. It's enough to drive anyone nuts, especially the poet herself. Prose poems, it seems, subvert the order. And what a relief! A prose poem at its best is like an empress who knows that when she is dressed in her best outfit, she is nude. And why not, I ask?

Why not love a nude empress?

When I was a fresh-woman in college, I complained to my English professor that poems often seemed pretentious. They reminded me of women in corsets with shrunken feet, or of old men in suits with cocktails and fake British accents. His response: our pretensions are all we are.

Sometimes I think he was right. From time to time, at least, a man needs pretensions. And clothes. A woman too. If nothing else they help define who a man is, just in case he or she forgets. Men are apt to do this from time to time. Women less so.

Women, it seems to me, suffer less from amnesia, and, without even noticing it, they cling more tightly to identity, form, clothes. Why?

Nin Andrews is the author of several books including *The Book of Orgasms* (2000), *Why They Grow Wings* (2001), *Midlife Crisis with Dick and Jane* (2005), *Dear Professor, Do You Live in a Vacuum?* (2008), and *Sleeping with Houdini* (2008). Her newest book, *Southern Comfort*, is just out from CavanKerry Press.

Because they are seen as such, i.e., as objects of art, sex, and style. Worse, they see themselves this way, starving their bodies, minds, and sometimes their poems and lives, too, into one form or another, depending on the culture or century. Maybe that's why I resist form so strongly. Why I can't stand anything that restricts my belly, feet, legs, arms, mind, muse. Or that tells me how to write and what to say.

I sometimes imagine all the women of the world rushing out into the night, waving their bare arms in the air and howling at the moon. I wonder if everyone feels as I do, that there is something essential I am forgetting, suppressing, wishing and dreaming, something more I could be writing and giving back to the world. But what?

Blaise Pascal always kept sewn in a special compartment of his coat, a little piece of paper to remind him of the two hours of life when he saw God. Maybe poets, too, need a coat, or at least a pocket or purse, for that sacred piece of paper on which to write the secrets gods tell them. After all, one never knows when the gods are going to start talking.

What if there is no coat? Is there then no poem? The same English professor from my first year in college informed me poetry must be in verse. Therefore prose poetry doesn't exist. He went on to say how much he liked it. He liked Robert Bly in particular. Of course he relabeled his work prose poetry with a slash through the word "poetry" but the word "poetry" remained, if only in shadow.

Like Bly I love the shadows of poetry. I love the shadows of tall trees and dreams and memories. I believe in these shadows, how they move and are constantly changing shapes. How sometimes I imagine I can feel the weight of my days leak a little from beneath my feet. Then I can see the distance between what I think and who I might be. Between what I say and what I mean.

Good things happen in those distances. Orgasms, for example. And wishes, prayers, and poems. Don't you think?

After all, poems are like orgasms. It's more our response to both of them that matters than the forms they take. And orgasms, too, have a shady reputation. Yet we never seem sure if they are real. If we have had them or not. Anxiously we question each other: did you . . . ? If only we could prove their existence. Then we could measure their wingspan, show them off for everyone to see. Maybe they'd look like angels or birds.

But I digress.

My favorite prayer is a prayer from St. Augustine: "O Lord, help me to be pure, but not yet."

My favorite poem is a darkly comic prose poem, "Simplicity," by the Belgian poet Henri Michaux. I translated it for the collection of Michaux poems that I edited called *Someone Wants to Steal My Name* (Cleveland State University Press, 2004).

Simplicity

What has been particularly lacking in my life up to now is simplicity. Little by little I am beginning to change.

For instance, I always go out with my bed now and when a woman pleases me, I take her and go to bed with her immediately.

If her ears are ugly and large, or her nose, I remove them along with her clothes and put them under the bed, for her to take back when she leaves; I keep only what I like.

If her underthings would improve by being changed, I change them immediately. This is my gift. But if I see a better-looking woman go by, I apologize to the first and make her disappear at once.

People who know me claim that I am incapable of doing what I have just described, that I haven't enough spunk. I once thought so myself, but that was because I was not then doing everything just as I pleased.

Now I always have excellent afternoons. (Mornings I work.)

Poems like this, full of laughter and insight, magic and perversity, are what make me fall in love with prose poetry again and again. They were my first loves and influences. And how could I resist? Their characters are as defective as I, and their humorous narratives inspire more than laughter. They reveal darker psychological truths. Like the voice of our shadows, they say what we deny yet know is so.

POEMS

About the Dead

It's true what they say about the dead. They don't just disappear, for example. They hang around for a while, amazed by what has passed. *I'm still here*, a girl might say to herself. She will think she's fine until she notices the living, or hears them.

Is she dead? one asks. *Yep, she's dead*, another answers.

A person can die again and again if she wants to, the girl learns. After all, there are so many ways of dying. Some die so slowly, they pass before they ever pass away. Others die like kamikaze pilots. Not a trace of them left, not even a wisp or a backward glance. Others shimmer and glow like sunsets on summer nights, putting on a show so everyone says oh and ah. Still others blink on and off like fireflies.

Crossing

Suppose the dead can't help looking back, pressing their wings against the glass like giant moths as if they don't get it, that the flesh is a cell, the light a 50 watt bulb. Maybe this dim life of regret is heaven after all. Like seeing you again at dusk, or imagining I do, there in the shadows of pines leaning through my windows, your arms waving in a frantic dance. When you kissed me, my back arcing like a bow, I remembered thinking the last kiss is always the best. I read that in a book about Tibetan monks who were paid to practice dying, to come back with news. After a while death became as familiar as a shirt slipped on or off. A kind of love affair, the monks discovered, an unspeakable intimacy. Some monks discovered a death that is just the right size, an ocean designed for the palms of their hands, each thimble-sized wave preparing for flight. Occasionally, one got stuck on the other side. Unable to touch the living or leave for good, he would call for help again and again, flailing his arms like the drowning, inhaling the ache in the distance between heaven and earth. I know how he felt, his silent cries, hot pebbles in the back of his throat.

Tung-Hui Hu

IT'S NOT IN CLEVELAND, BUT I'M GETTING CLOSER

I wrote my first prose poem in a hurry. My friend was about to walk through the door, but also, magnolias were blooming around me—I wasn't sure how long that would last. I didn't have time for line breaks.

I wrote that poem on a postcard, and I've been trying to work out if the two forms are connected. Perhaps a lyric poem can be compared to a letter, where reader and author enter into a relationship of reciprocity. But prose poems and postcards address us differently. A postcard's message is often flat and self-referential: "I'm here… wish you were here!" I've gone through old postcards sold at flea markets, and the words tend to resemble each other; even the handwriting begins to look the same. Hoping to find something prurient, I'll touch what other people have touched, but I'm frustrated. It's the opposite of seduction: Having it, but still not knowing what it is—rifling through jackets in the hallway rather than lingerie in the drawer.

I like this style of address, though, because it doesn't presume anything: It doesn't solicit a reply. Instead, a good prose poem makes its own envelope. It wraps and secrets words inside a block of text, rather than unfolding meaning outwards onto the page (the Latin *implicare* rather than *explicare*). And what I like to read looks like the careless text you might encounter walking down the street, on the side of buildings, or in a newspaper. Without a wrapper to contain the words or set them apart

Tung-Hui Hu is the author of two books of poetry, *Mine* (2007) and *The Book of Motion* (2003); his writing has also appeared in *The New Republic, Ploughshares, Gastronomica,* and *Martha Stewart Living Radio*. His latest project is a sound installation titled *The Last Time You Cried* (lasttimeyoucried.com). A native of San Francisco, he currently teaches at the University of Michigan.

from the everyday, the images of a good prose poem appear to be cut out of the world.

Also, a prose poem must convince you that it's a poem. Without obvious indicators, such as white space, a reader must decide for him or herself what the poetic qualities are. Although a prose poem seems formless—seems like it discards rules altogether—I think a prose poem is as much a product of constraint as a villanelle or a sonnet. A series of withouts: without line breaks, without interruption.

As with the white space of a postcard that restricts the writing surface, a prose poem is fragmentary. Nothing stops a lyric poem from going on indefinitely; the temporality of a lyric poem is endless. But a prose poem has to stop; too long and it turns into a short story. (I'm not sure about the opposite, though: Would the shortest prose poem be one line?) A postcard is, like the photograph that hangs on its side, an instant, an excerpt from a larger story. This frame produces smallness, "hereness": A prose poem is a thought made portable. Half the time it won't even end properly, leaving you unsure when you'll get a chance to see another one; but this form—repetitive and too brief, all at once—produces an episodic sense of time.

Something happens when you read through enough postcards, when enough instants accumulate. A bar close to me, Specs Twelve Adler Place, has a galvanized metal bin filled with a decade's worth of postcards. Many of them have been sent by the same person. He writes: "I'm looking for the American dream. It's not in Cleveland, but I'm getting closer." Or, later, "In Arizona. Just missed it, though I think I caught a glimpse." Corners are bent and splitting; edges are well thumbed. For me, these postcards make an extended prose poem, one that disappears from and reappears into the thick of the stack. Together, photographs of waves, grain silos, and canyons suggest that their author is somewhere out in the world, and you are not. He is searching for the extended story measured in decades, the story that endures silently behind the poem.

POEMS

Lisboa, 1755

The day the earthquake came capsizing even the battleships in the bay I was watching João Manuel de Lourenço fashion a ring out of some inscrutable alloy he had fished out with a gleam in his eyes and which I secretly named adamantite. This ring I was to use to court Isabel Amorim and that she would resist my advances a fifth time was unfathomable: on this point my jeweler assented wholly. For he could feel each mineral as an organ swelling inside the earth and as we spoke had even begun to taste the metal, biting the gold as if he could feel its softness. Consequently the links and chains he fashioned were not to bind the neck or the ankle but for the sadness and melancholy that one carries like a worn passport. But even as he worked I heard the bells of the church outside give a terrible groan and burst, and I thought Senhor de Lourenço had fallen off his chair, only it was the earth that gave way, the drawers splaying open to reveal a strange light of metals. And as he fumbled around on the floor as an overturned tortoise flails its legs it was then I realized the man was blind, this man whom I had grown to trust better than my own hands.

Five Dollars

She tells you to bring her five dollars. You go home. You look for change in the couch. You bring it to her. She turns off the light. You lie in the dark with your clothes off. Nobody moves. You have seen geese stunned after flying into a glass window: it is the same thing with your bodies. You hope something will change color. You hope it is something uprooted inside of you. You start to worry someone will find you still there the next morning. Your neck is beginning to get sore. You say Is that it? She says Yeah, that's what it is. The lights go on. You look down. It is the dew that appears after a summer night.

Mary Ann Samyn

"CLOSE TO YOU"
The Prose Poem: Some Observations

When I consider things that put me under their spell, prose poems come to mind. So does Karen Carpenter. I remember, and like, a lot of the music from the 1970s: my childhood. But I sang only The Carpenters' songs in my basement in Royal Oak, Michigan, in what was then the center of the world.

~

Every time I begin to write about prose poems, I end up writing a prose poem. Which just goes to show.

~

When I first wrote prose poems, my classmates and teacher told me that I was still writing the line. I took this as a compliment. What better friend for a poet than the line? We walked arm and arm: crook in crook.

~

Then, the bend was the thing. Crook in crook. The angle. Enjambment. Somewhere along the way, however, the path straightened. Now I'm much less likely to write an enjambed line. Whereas once I was all about the comma, now I like a full stop. One thing at a time.

~

Now, I respect the sentence too.

~

If the white space is otherwise occupied, and it is, then the lined poem and the prose poem are two expressions of the opposite of that occupa-

Mary Ann Samyn is the author of five collections of poetry, most recently *Beauty Breaks In* (2009), *Purr* (2005), and *Inside the Yellow Dress* (2001). She teaches in the MFA program at West Virginia University where she also holds the Bolton Professorship for Teaching and Mentoring.

tion. By *occupation* I mean "livelihood, vocation" not "invasion." Don't get carried away.

~

Today's prose poem featured Karen Carpenter on lead vocals and Richard on piano. You remember them. You remember at least some of the words. Admit it.

~

But why is Karen a prose poem, and why do I feel at liberty to call her Karen, and where did I put my tambourine?

~

Something has been breached. As when a dam breaks and we have to call the Army Corps of Engineers.

~

Practicalities aside, the prose poem does direct the flow differently than a lined poem. "Practicalities aside" is just a phrase I like to say. In real life, I use my hands to direct the flow. No, really. I move my hands to open the poem, or keep it open, or say *you're closed—*.

~

Let the white space be your guide.

~

Liberty is a big idea with several definitions. I, however, do not "take liberties with chronology" or "take foolish liberties on the ski slopes," but I do write prose poems.

~

Believe it or not, Karen Carpenter is not among the famous people listed in my *American Heritage Dictionary*. Surely, this is an oversight.

~

If we could inhabit the scenic lookout of the prose poem, we could oversee the white space. Though, no, we could not supervise it; in that you are correct.

~

Was this the "watershed moment" the editors mentioned?

~

It's not my process that differs; it's the push and pull of language. Magnets are a useful metaphor. In many of my lined poems, there is a strong sense of each line existing independently and, indeed, repelling, to some extent, the other lines. In my prose poems, the attraction is much stronger. That cohesive force holds the prose poem together and accounts for its blockiness. Yet, there is something happening sentence to sentence.

~

As though a bucket has been lowered into each *between*…

~

The most powerful prose poems conjure more than one mood. Another bucket lowered.

~

I think it's telling that I've had one of my favorite prose poem anthologies, *Models of the Universe*, disappear on more than one occasion. I lend it; it doesn't come back. Eventually, I track it down or get another, but always there is this sense that the book inspires theft. Now that's a compliment.

~

In one of my all-time favorite prose poems, "How to Make Poison," Margaret Atwood writes what I consider one of the truest things ever: "People like to make poison. If you don't understand this you will never understand anything."

~

Every poem we write is an example of what we believe about poetry. Probably also about life. If it isn't, then you and I don't write poetry the same way.

~

When I sang those songs in my basement, I was not interested in being, or being like, Karen Carpenter. That would not have occurred to me. Rather, I was, and remain, interested in being more like me.

~

The inimitable among us teach us how to be inimitable.

~

That prose poems have a reputation for being quirky is, of course, part of their appeal. Failed prose poems, though, are only quirky and are perhaps more susceptible to this failing than are lined poems. The best prose poems are quirky plus. The former are quick and cheap; the latter tell us something about how it feels to live.

~

I was taught, and learned, that "all questions are formal questions," thus I consider the method of delivery to be the message delivered.

~

Perhaps this is the difference: in my lined poems, I expect to have to wait, exposed, out in the open; in my prose poems, I push a button and the elevator opens and then I go up or down, depending.

~

A good thing to do when you're inside a prose poem is look around. If you can do that, you'll be okay.

~

The best poems say, *crouch here; wait with me.* Or, *push a button; you choose; it's scary-fun.*

~

But my favorite elevator button is not a button to push but a button that lights up: "Help is on the way."

~

In the song "Close to You," Karen Carpenter sings about the day the angels conspired, dreaming up your birth. If this were a poem, we might consider how the "you" might be both another person and the speaker addressing herself. Poems make such considerations possible. And it's a good thing, I think, to imagine angels in cahoots. Perhaps this is the beginning of a charmed life.

~

A charm is something we can possess as a trait or object. We can be held under the sway of someone else's charm. We can use a charm to ward off evil. Trinket, incantation, fascination. There's even a quantum property called charm that is related to longevity and strangeness in quarks. All memorable poems, I'd argue, are charming in one or more of these ways. Prose poems, too, have their charms, and I, for one, have been susceptible.

~

Have I answered your questions charmingly? I wonder.

~

I will say this: no matter the poem, I work off titles and/or beginnings. Not ideas, mind you (ha!), but language. The surest way to write a bad poem is to set out with something important to say. Better to begin with a little string of willingness. This is my process, regardless.

~

About-ness is not a big concern. If I get fidgety, I just play my tambourine.

~

Also, I write my poems as they appear on the page; that is, I don't impose a shape after the fact. The shape is the fact. Part and parcel.

~

Most of my failed poems are the result of not being able to discover (hear) the shape that will deliver. Most of my advice to myself is "listen harder."

~

Finally, what I know is this: The best poems, prose or otherwise, cannot be explained in an essay. Explicate all you like, but something essential—something deeply charming—will not yield to analysis, thank goodness.

~

Do I consider the prose poem's future? Sorry, no. Do I consider my own? Yes, indeed.

⌒⁄⁄⌒

POEMS
from The Little Book of Female Mystics

—Can't you see that I am not the person I was? Time is no more than the point of a needle. Same goes for suffering. Once I said, "Always eat your protein first." And mostly I got stronger. Now knowledge grows more intense, and lustrous as a pelt. Not all visionary experiences are created equal; Catherine of Siena and Christ exchanged hearts. The sadness of church is the sadness of what could have been. The sadness of me, ditto. I am not wishing to be an anchoress. I am not counting on anything. I am remembering learning to swim—no metaphor—at the Bambi Motel, Sault Sainte Marie, Michigan. If this is pride, then sometimes I too am amazed my soul stays in my body. Does God monitor such thoughts? I'm thinking not.

Wish You Were Here

Postcard of time, stolen time. And I have such wide need. How can I tell you of all the birds visiting me? First, geese at night—just as you said—flying by the light of the river. No, I mean by the absence of the light of the river. Then, cranes, three: a dream, a painting, a photograph. Also, this paper if you fold it: origami sign of—what? Good fortune against great distances, against exhaustion, or so I've read. Remember, you said you wanted birds at parting. Okay then, take mine. Let this be the feather in your mailbox.

Maxine Chernoff

FORM AND FUNCTION
Language in a Double World

According to Russian psychologist Alexander Luria, "With the help of language [humans] can deal with things they have not perceived even indirectly and with things which were part of the experience of older generations. This ability adds another dimension to the world of humans. . . . Animals have only one world, the world of objects and situations which can be perceived by the senses. Humans have a double world." In choosing verse or the prose poem, I am trying to accommodate my register of this double world to the form that best suits it. If I am thinking (or dreaming) of a world of objects that float in proximity to each other and create odd connections, as in the Frank O'Hara poem "Steps," where two people pass each other and their "surgical implements lock for a day," then the best medium for that accidental conjunction is the prose poem. Many of my earliest prose poems written under the influence of masters such as Michaux, Cortazar, Lispector, Jacob, Cendrars, Calvino (and the list continues) work in that mode. It is as if the poem were conditional, "if X happens or should happen, then. . ." The prose poem gives me liberty to explore the accidental meetings, the space in which a fan speaks to an anonymous man who enters a room, or an artist designs a windmill of famous moustaches, or bridges of perishable items are erected to console man about mortal-

Maxine Chernoff is the author of six collections of fiction and ten collections of poetry, of which *A Vegetable Emergency* (1976), *Utopia TV Store* (1979), *New Faces of 1952* (1985), and *Evolution of the Bridge* (2004) were books of prose poems. She is chair of Creative Writing at San Francisco State University, and with Paul Hoover, edits *New American Writing* and has translated *The Selected Poems of Friedrich Hoeliderlin*, which won the PEN USA Translation Award.

ity. I wanted a space in which I could explore the image and sustain its intensity with a deadpan speaker reporting on such events.

Later I moved to the prose poem to capture dialogue between speakers in a manner that respected the lengths and patterns of human utterance. These more recent prose poems, which are most often arguments between a man and a woman and have been adapted into a play by Mac Maginnes and staged at Small Press Traffic's Poets' Theater Festival in San Francisco, are terse and tense language duets that need the ragged borders and sentence patterns of prose. Were I to pay attention to line break or overly control rhythm, it would undermine the ebb and flow of the dialogue and truncate the human speech which strives to be realistic. These poems record social moments, often discord or misunderstanding and require an expansive form, which prose poems allow perhaps more easily than verse.

My other two more recent efforts have been in verse. The first is a series of poems based on "Gift Theory," which analyzes social relations through the literal and symbolic exchange of gifts and includes such important figures as Mauss, Godelier, Derrida, Emerson, and Irigaray, among others. My interest here was to extract a narrow, sinuous sonically constructed poem from far longer non-poetic essays. It was a process of losing words or erasure that led to narrow poems that tumbled down the page such as the fragment below based on an essay by Godelier:

> [one in space, the other in time]
> I need opacity
>   to see myself—
> through prayers
>   & sacrifice
> as I exist
>   it is my wish
>   to make
>   a world
> through laws
> and then
> to miss
>
>   the recognition. . .

My goal in extracting the essay's argument and in some poems providing a counterargument is to contemplate all aspects of the gift as an economy and a vehicle for ethics. The uneven vertical columns of words serve to emphasize individual phrases, juxtapose them to others, and maintain sonic connections and segues. Prose would not be adept at achieving the type of visual highlighting needed for words and phrases to be isolated and take on a proper weight, nor would it allow for the quickness with which I feel these arguments moving, almost as if they are a liquid medium being poured through a funnel.

Having been pleased with my results in my "reading through" projects, I have again explored that possibility in a long poem that locates sentences in individual texts and joins them together with anaphora using the female pronouns she or her. The poem, now six pages long, explores "she" sentences in a variety of contexts from literary fiction to commercial fiction to prose essays in areas including economics, philosophy, art, and literary theory. I have found in beginning this project that there is a paucity of "she" sentences in most theoretical writing, so I have also given myself permission to change the arbitrary subject of a sentence from "he" to "she" when I so choose. Since I want the repeated word at the beginning of many sentences (such as the words "I saw," which open most lines of Ginsberg's *Howl*), I am writing in extremely long lines that seem to break down the borders between poetry and prose—hence I am approaching prose poem form once again with lines blurring almost into prose but from a different starting point. Here is a section of my poem, "He Picked Up His Pen in Her Defense":

> She had done a great wrong. Over a dozen people suffered.
> She was said to sweat literature.
> Marriage suited her better than nakedness.
> Her fingers curled around the bone of his hip.
> She stood statue-like at the foot of the scaffold.
> I loved her so much that I was glad to do it all.
> The girl was Miss Chadwick, and she was from the South.
> I imagined her young, raging, tearing at her bodice. . . .

In my case, then, the purpose, texture, speed, and sound of the writing seem to determine the form I choose, whether prose poem or verse.

When I want more constraints, I will most often choose verse. When I want a dreamy exploration of objects and images or the ragged shapes of human speech, prose has served me better. Moreover, each project arrives with its own logic and constraints. I try to honor their inherent logic by choosing the form which best suits it.

I came to prose poems very early and was the only woman I knew of writing them in the early to mid-70s when my prose poems appeared in two collections in 1976 (*The Last Aurochs* and *A Vegetable Emergency*). My relationship with the form has all the characteristics of any long relationship—with periods of enchantment and disenchantment. Over the years as I've written other forms (including short stories and the novel), I have sometimes felt impatient or unsympathetic with prose poems for their lightness and whimsy. At other times I've returned to early masters or encountered them in life, as I did Russell Edson at a recent reading in New York, and been reminded of their unique resiliency. Poets such as Rosmarie Waldrop as well have convinced me of how the prose poem can balance vision with seriousness and be used to investigate intimate states of mind.

POEMS
Heavenly Bodies
—When is that huge meteor scheduled to hit Earth?

—I heard something about 2035.

—You mean in thirty-seven years the world might end?

—The world wouldn't end.

—If a meteor of that size hits Earth, we'll be destroyed.

—We might be destroyed, but there'd still be a world.

—Do you mean a universe?

—I guess that's what I mean.

—How will there be a universe if we're not there to form the concept?

—Do you think we're so important that the whole universe can't exist if we don't? What was here before we were born?

—History was here.

—That's exactly it. We're simply a part of it all, like a whorl in a tree trunk.

—Why didn't you say a grain of sand on a beach?

—Okay, a grain of sand on a beach.

—How can someone who knows so much about the universe be persuaded to use a cliché?

—Death is a cliché.

—What do you mean?

—It's given to us, and we can do nothing to change it.

—But you're saying our own deaths don't matter. Not now. Not in thirty-seven years, not if the universe gets destroyed.

—Exactly.

—So what should we do?

—About what?

—What should we do to prevent the meteor from destroying us?

—I guess we could intercept it.

—Who, you and me?

—The government.

—I knew it.

—Knew what?

—You're some kind of hired assassin.

—What do you mean?

—You're hired by the government to make me think I don't matter, not even if I die.

—How does that make me an assassin?

—It's conceptual. You erase me with your thoughts.

—So maybe I'm more of an artist than an assassin.

—How much do they pay you?

—Who?

—The government.

—Why would the government hire me to convince you of anything? Is either of us so important?

—Here you go again. You just won't admit it.

—Admit what?

—That when we die the universe will perish.

—Okay. When we die the universe will perish. Does that make you feel better?

—Yes, momentarily.

Subtraction

First there was addition, incestuous and pretentious, coupling jackals with jackals, summing sunsets and field mice. Soon the world was packed as a third class railway car. We tired of objects desiring us—lenses, doorknobs, cuspidors elbowing between lovers. Scholars developed protective philosophies, claiming they'd die for "breathing space," but what of the common man? His only hope was in the invention of madmen—evaporation chambers, metaphysical vacuums, all of which failed. One day in a schoolroom a slow child with glasses forgot to draw the vertical line of the plus sign and so subtraction was born. *Minus, minus*, we chanted all day, watching our laundry recede from the clothesline.

Carol Guess

THOUGHTS ON PROSE BLOCKS AS DANCE AND RESISTANCE

Writing this, looking out this particular window at a paper mill and a parking garage, I'm not married. I was married once, and I'm not divorced, but neither am I married at this moment. It's a puzzle, isn't it? The pieces don't fit. To find the answer you must cross the border.

Take a right from my house. Turn left at the light. Take the long low road until it hits the highway. Take the highway across the Canadian border. Here, in Vancouver, I'm married again.

In Vancouver, my love and I are bound together. In Washington, we're severed; not even annulled, simply disappeared. Which is to say that the stakes in naming are high. To name a thing is to allow it entry into your world. To refuse to name it means to refuse to see it; or, subversively, to refuse to acquiesce to interpellation.

Start again: It's possible for me to tell a different kind of story about prose poetry. To describe the constant tension I experience between the impulse to make meaning and the impulse to focus on sound alone, on letters as musical notation. In this story I don't know what I'm looking for, but when I find it, my heart beats faster. In this story the two novels that were my first books feel far away; I can't find enough uninterrupted space to complete another novel. After a decade of teaching full time, beaten down a little by all that comes with the struggle for tenure, I decide to stop. Stop trying to squeeze my life into a form that doesn't fit. I decide to abandon traditional forms and squeeze everything—unfin-

Carol Guess' fifth book, the prose poetry collection *Tinderbox Lawn*, was published by Rose Metal Press in 2008. Previous books include *Seeing Dell* (1996), *Switch* (1998), *Gaslight* (2001), and *Femme's Dictionary* (2004). She is an associate professor of English at Western Washington University, where she teaches creative writing and queer studies.

ished novels, stories, essays, poems, fragments—into tiny, tight blocks. Compression creates an unexpectedly playful, pleasurable process. What's unsaid matters as much as what's said. By narrowing my vision I've created a different kind of beauty. Because I'm working in such small spaces, I have enough time to make each line musical. That music matters more to me now than stretching time across the page.

It makes sense, then—this movement from novels to prose blocks. But how to explain why I'm not using line breaks, white space, fragments as often as I did in my first book of poetry? That's harder to explain, even to myself. I think it has to do with wanting to create a specific sort of sound. This, too, ties back to place. When I moved to the Pacific Northwest from the East Coast, Deep South, Great Plains, and Midwest, I was entranced by the music I found here—Sleater-Kinney, Elliott Smith, Laura Veirs, The Gossip. A DIY aesthetic links these sounds, but there's something else, too. A long breath, exhaled. I think of New York City as a gasp. The South was held in, and the Great Plains, hardened. I want to write sentences that involve the body: lots of falling, a curved spine, propulsion. A prose block is dance; it's also a compressed novel (a novel the writer doesn't have time to write) and a rogue lyric (a song the writer hopes will never end).

> The clerk rolled each finger through ink onto paper, rather like making music together. Crossing out groom, writing bride #2. Nobody notices us, but we do.

✐

POEMS

Primer

Hand-over-heart-ish I was just small. I couldn't say stuff slowly, like the bunch. Satin patches on puffy cuffs. My smile silver. Never used an eraser. The alphabet smooshed: *Elemento-P*. Love came later than I would have liked. Came with a price. Came with prey and dominion. Came to stain my floor vermilion and my back door torque. Came as hard work. Valentines flew point-first into the shredder. Fashioned a petticoat, *ahem* at hem. Wrought-iron birds guarded my skirt, iron flocks floating on the freeway's breeze. Some birds returned, but some went missing, building nests out of condoms and keys.

The Belltown Angel

In place of solitude I see the sky. Across the city someone holds dinner for a dozen high above his head. Traffic becomes maps of traffic becomes voices on the radio talking about traffic. Someone holds loaves of bread to her chest and kicks open a wooden door with her boot.

Everything we've lost has been returned to us for this day only. Everything is on sale and the air quality has never been better.

Hostages shiver in the shadow of my burnt-out buildings. Lovers and night dreamers leave icons at my feet, so many candles to drowsy Maria and African Jesus. I sign an animal pact to the lost souls who kneel to me. I sing a lullaby to the glittery drunks and bedraggled drag queens who parade beneath my fiberglass wings. The sky splits into heartstars that guide strippers home, spindly shoes draped over their shoulders, thighs smelling of shaving cream and dollar bills. I spread my wings over the forge where the black dog sleeps, over the corner where a man reads Lorca to his homeless lover.

David Shumate

BOTH RIVERS

Nowadays it suits me to write at the confluence of prose and poetry, one foot in each stream, sampling the waters of each. But I'm not on a crusade to promote the prose poem. Crusades are a tricky business. They require lots of heavy gear. Sharp weapons. Horses. Gothic banners proclaiming the cause. Knights with silly names. Holy texts that weigh more than all the rest combined. By the time you get where you're headed, you forget why you came.

Besides, tomorrow I might take after Issa and write only in Haiku.

~

In high school I became intrigued by Sherwood Anderson's *Winesburg, Ohio*. His little book of grotesques. Later I came across Richard Brautigan's lyrical prose—*In Watermelon Sugar* and *Trout Fishing in America*. I still wonder how such beauty is legal.

I was entranced by the Tang Dynasty poets—Tu Fu and Wang Wei and others. Kenneth Rexroth and Arthur Waley rendered them strangely contemporary, as if they were American poets who got drunk one night and stowed away on a ship to the Orient.

It all mixed together. Lyrical prose. Poems extolling the enchantment of the ordinary.

I came across the prose poem about 30 years ago in Robert Bly's translations of Federico Garcia Lorca and Juan Ramon Jiménez. I was

David Shumate is the author of *High Water Mark* (2004), winner of the 2003 Agnes Lynch Starrett Prize, and *The Floating Bridge* (2008). His poetry has appeared widely in literary journals and has been anthologized in *The Writer's Almanac*, *Good Poems for Hard Times*, and *The Best American Poetry 2007*. He is the recipient of a 2009 NEA Poetry Fellowship. He teaches at Marian University in Indianapolis and lives in Zionsville, Indiana.

intrigued by Jiménez's prose poems, and later by *Platero y Yo*. I read and enjoyed Bly's own *Morning Glory*.

~

I began to compose prose poems, but I was soon seduced by fiction. I returned to the prose poem 20 years later looking for an intensity, a compression that fiction didn't afford.

In truth, I'm drawn to the prose poem's homeliness. Its inelegance. Like a bulbous dirigible there on the page. I like to see if I can make it float away in defiance of all poetic gravity.

Lately, I've found myself writing what might be called prose sonnets, prose poems of about fourteen lines, give or take a half dozen. Like their traditional counterparts, they tend to present a problem, turn toward a resolution, and seal the deal with the last few lines. "After They Plundered the Language" is one of those, a few lines short of being the genuine article.

~

The poems I'm most drawn to possess a kind of transparency. They dissolve a little as you read them until all that remains is a faint glow on the other side.

Many of my poems end up being centered between two worlds. Only occasionally do they contain elements that betray their place in time. Their decade or century. I am most comfortable in that thin slice of the poetic world layered between the mythic and the mundane. It requires less maintenance. And the taxes are lower there.

~

The prose poem is often the object of derision among poetic purists. They consider the loss of the poetic line a final blasphemy. They've relinquished rhyme. And meter. But never the line itself. They claim a poem must be vertical. A poem must look like a poem.

Maybe they're right. Maybe there is a special purgatory for our kind. Perhaps I'm already a resident there. That would explain a lot…

But I've overheard some fairly comical conversations between poets concerning the proper placement of a line break. Should it go here? Or here? Or here? Often it comes just to the brink of fisticuffs. Then the poet goes off and reads the poem to an audience, completely ignoring the line breaks he fought so hard to justify. Often if they do read their own line breaks rigidly, the overall effect can be a sort of literary stutter as if there might be a sudden shortage of air in the room.

~

I primarily use the lantern of intuition when I write prose poems. I begin with little sense of the complete poem. I start out with an image. A title. An echo of sounds. Then I feel my way along. I'm usually surprised where I end up.

Many of my subjects are based on a real experience that has mutated over time. I began "Taking the Psychological Test" with a faint recollection of seeing my first set of Rorschach images and thinking how odd it seemed that a person's sanity might be determined by one's reaction to blotches on a page. The speaker of the poem seemed to want to enter a session with a psychologist wielding this tool and engage in a little battle of wits with him. At the time I didn't know about the camel that was lurking at the end of the poem in the doctor's doodling. Or the amorous couple, for that matter. But what may be the best parts of a poem usually take us by surprise.

~

My poems assume their final shape after a long process of distillation. I remove anything I can. I try to coax them to shed their winter fat. When they begin to take over more than a quarter of the page, I become anxious. Why is this taking so long?

I have noticed a tendency in some modern prose poems to lean heavily toward the prosaic side at the expense of their lyricism. They become long, languid stories. They don't pursue their glowing core but instead chat on and on.

I don't know what the future holds for the genre. I hope that in time the prose poem will find its own space, maybe somewhere in the basement of the poetic world. Down there where the children and old folks go to be alone. Down there where all the secrets of the house are stored.

POEMS

After They Plundered the Language

We noticed their campfires up in the hills but thought they belonged to shepherds. Then one night the barbarians swooped down while we were sleeping and made off with a thousand precious words. Like the one we spoke at burials to usher the dead into the dark. And those phrases we learned from the Greeks who in turn stole them from the gods. And all those words lovers invented on their own. They, too, have vanished. Only the words of commerce and utility remain. Sometimes we're reduced to drawing pictures to convey what we mean. Or gesturing with our hands There used to be a gentle word we spoke when we wanted to be intimate with a lover. It conveyed both desire and good faith. Now we must paint our faces red. Do a little dance. And set a hat by her door.

Taking the Psychological Test

The psychologist asks me to consider the black spot smeared across his paper and tell him what I see. It is, indeed, a strange phenomenon. And I can see why he's concerned. I, too, would be perplexed if I found something like that lying on my desk. I ask him how it got there. *A pervert, perhaps? Or a vandal with no respect for private property?* He suggests I simply focus on what it looks like to me. So I tell him that it's one of those muffled explosions that happens in the mind as happiness turns to sadness. I point to its jagged outline. And all that debris scattered about. I show him the glowing core that once was pure joy and ask him how he managed to photograph it. He turns the paper around and studies the blotch as if he's never thought of this before which seems odd since he's the doctor and I'm the patient and he should know these kinds of things. I notice the doodling on his notepad that looks like two people lost in the throes of love while riding backwards on a camel. But I hesitate to mention the fact.

FURTHER READING

The contributors, editors, and press recommend the following:

ANTHOLOGIES

Alexander, Robert, C.W. Truesdale and Mark Vinz, eds. *The Party Train: A Collection of North American Prose Poetry*. Buffalo, NY: White Pine Press, 1996.

Alexander, Robert and Dennis Maloney, eds. *The House of Your Dream*. Buffalo, NY: White Pine Press, 2008.

Benedikt, Michael, ed. *The Prose Poem: An International Anthology*. New York: Dell, 1977.

Bly, Robert, ed. *Lorca and Jimenez: Selected Poems*. Boston, MA: Beacon Press, 2007.

Clements, Brian and Jamey Dunham, eds. *An Introduction to the Prose Poem*. Danbury, CT: Firewheel Editions, 2009.

Conners, Peter, ed. *PP/FF: An Anthology*. Buffalo, NY: Starcherone Books, 2006.

Friebert, Stuart and David Young, eds. *Models of the Universe: An Anthology of the Prose Poem*. Oberlin, OH: Oberlin College Press, 1995.

Lehman, David, ed. *Great American Prose Poems: From Poe to the Present*. New York: Scribner, 2003.

Maloney, Dennis, ed. *Dreaming the Miracle: Three French Prose Poets: Max Jacob, Jean Follain, Francis Ponge*. Buffalo, NY: White Pine Press, 2002.

Meyers Jr., George, ed. *Epiphanies: The Prose Poem Now*. Toronto: Cumberland Press, 1987.

Millman, Lawrence, ed. *A Kayak Full of Ghosts: Eskimo Tales*. Northampton, MA: Interlink Books, 2003.

CRITICAL WORKS

Bachelard, Gaston. *The Poetics of Space*. Boston, MA: Beacon Press, 1994.

Delville, Michel. *The American Prose Poem: Poetic Form and the Boundaries of Genre*. Gainsville, FL: University Press of Florida, 1998.

Iglesias, Holly. *Boxing Inside the Box: Women's Prose Poetry*. Williamsburg, MA: Quale Press, 2004.

SINGLE-AUTHOR COLLECTIONS

Alexander, Robert. *What the Raven Said*. Buffalo, NY: White Pine Press, 2006.

Alexander, Robert. *White Pine Sucker*. Minneapolis, MN: New Rivers Press, 1993.

Aliesan, Jody. *True North/Nord Vrai*. Yakima, WA: Blue Begonia Press, 2006.

Anderson, Jack. *Traffic*. Buffalo, NY: White Pine Press, 2000.

Andrews, Nin. *The Book of Orgasms*. Cleveland, OH: Cleveland State University Poetry Center, 2000.

Andrews, Tom. *Random Symmetries: The Collected Poems of Tom Andrews*. Oberlin, OH: Oberlin College Press, 2002.

Ashbery, John. *Three Poems*. New York: Ecco Press, 1989.

Baudelaire, Charles. *Paris Spleen*. New York: New Directions, 1970.

Baus, Eric. *The To Sound*. Seattle, WA: Verse Press, 2004.

Baus, Eric. *Tuned Droves*. Portland, OR: Octopus Books, 2009.

Benedikt, Michael. *Sky*. Middletown, CT: Wesleyan University Press, 1970.

Bly, Robert. *Reaching Out to the World: New and Selected Prose Poems*. Buffalo, NY: White Pine Press, 2009.

Bly, Robert. *The Morning Glory: Prose Poems*. New York: HarperCollins, 1975.

Bonomo, Joe. *Installations*. New York: Penguin, 2008.

Borzutzky, Daniel. *The Ecstasy of Capitulation*. Buffalo, NY: BlazeVOX Books, 2006.

Boully, Jenny. *The Body*. Ithaca, NY: Essay Press, 2007.

Bradley, John. *Add Musk Here*. Montpelier, OH: Pavement Saw Press, 2002.

Brainard, Joe. *I Remember*. New York: Granary Books, 2001.

Broumas, Olga and Jane Miller. *Black Holes, Black Stockings*. Middletown, CT: Wesleyan University Press, 1985.

Brouwer, Joel. *Centuries*. New York: Four Way Books, 2003.

Buckley, Christopher. *Modern History*. North Adams, MA: Tupelo Press, 2008.

Byrd, Brigitte. *Fence above the Sea*. Boise, ID: Ahsahta Press, 2005.

Byrd, Brigitte. *Song of a Living Room*. Boise, ID: Ahsahta Press, 2009.

Byrne, Mairead. *Talk Poetry*. Miami, OH: Miami University Press, 2007.

Carson, Anne. *Glass, Irony and God*. New York: New Directions, 1995.

Carsten, Rene Nielsen. Trans. David Keplinger. *World Cut Out with Crooked Scissors: Selected Prose Poems*. Kalamazoo, MI: New Issues Press, 2007.

Chernoff, Maxine. *Evolution of the Bridge*. London: Salt Publishing, 2004.

Clary, Killarney. *By Common Salt*. Oberlin, OH: Oberlin College Press, 1996.

Clary, Killarney. *By Me, By Any, Can and Can't Be Done*. Santa Cruz, CA: Greenhouse Review Press, 1980.

Clary, Killarney. *Potential Stranger*. Chicago: University of Chicago Press, 2003.

Clary, Killarney. *Who Whispered Near Me*. New York: Farrar, Straus and Giroux, 1989.

Conners, Peter. *Of Whiskey and Winter*. Buffalo, NY: White Pine Press, 2007.

Cortázar, Julio. *Cronopios and Famas*. New York: New Directions, 1999.

Coultas, Brenda. *The Marvelous Bones of Time: Excavations and Explanations*. Minneapolis, MN: Coffee House Press, 2007.

Daniel, David. *Seven-Star Bird*. Minneapolis, MN: Graywolf Press, 2003.

Debeljak, Aleš. Trans. Christopher Merrill. *Anxious Moments*. Buffalo, NY: White Pine Press, 1995.

Duhamel, Denise. *Mille et un sentiments*. Danbury, CT: Firewheel Editions, 2005.

Duhamel, Denise. *The Star-Spangled Banner*. Carbondale, IL: Southern Illinois University Press, 1999.

Edson, Russell. *The Tunnel: Selected Prose Poems*. Oberlin, OH: Oberlin College Press, 1994.

Eimers, Nancy. *A Grammar to Waking*. Pittsburgh, PA: Carnegie Mellon University Press, 2005.

Fixel, Lawrence. *Truth, War and the Dream Game*. Minneapolis, MN: Coffee House Press, 1991.

Follain, Jean. *A World Rich in Anniversaries*. Durango, CO: Logbridge-Rhodes, 1981.

Galeano, Eduardo. *The Book of Embraces*. New York: W.W. Norton, 1992.

Galeano, Eduardo. *Memory of Fire Trilogy*. New York: W.W. Norton, 1998.

Gibbon, Maureen. *Magdalena*. Buffalo, NY: White Pine Press, 2006.

Goldberg, Beckian Fritz. *Lie Awake Lake*. Oberlin, OH: Oberlin College Press, 2005.

Gonzalez, Ray. *Cool Auditor*. Rochester, NY: BOA Editions, 2009.

Goodman, Loren. *Famous Americans*. New Haven, CT: Yale University Press, 2003.

Greenberg, Arielle. *Given*. Amherst, MA: Verse Press, 2002.

Griffith, Kevin. *Denmark, Kangaroo, Orange*. Long Beach, CA: Pearl Editions, 2007.

Guess, Carol. *Tinderbox Lawn*. Brookline, MA: Rose Metal Press, 2008.

Harms, James. *After West*. Pittsburgh, PA: Carnegie Mellon University Press, 2008.

Harrison, Jim. *Letters to Yesenin*. Port Townsend, WA: Copper Canyon Press, 2007.

Harvey, Matthea. *Modern Life*. Minneapolis, MN: Graywolf Press, 2007.

Hass, Robert. *Human Wishes*. New York: Ecco Press, 1990.

Hejinian, Lyn. *My Life*. Los Angeles, CA: Green Integer Books, 2002.

Herbert, Zbigniew. *The Collected Poems: 1956-1998*. New York: Ecco Press, 2009.

Hicok, Bob. *This Clumsy Living*. Pittsburgh, PA: University of Pittsburgh Press, 2007.

Hu, Tung-Hui. *Mine*. Keene, NY: Ausable Press, 2007.

Iglesias, Holly. *Souvenirs of a Shrunken World*. Tucson, AZ: Kore Press, 2008.

Jacob, Max. Trans. John Ashbery. *The Dice Cup: Selected Prose Poems*. St. Paul, MN: Bookslinger, 1980.

Jarman, Mark. *Epistles*. Louisville, KY: Sarabande Books, 2007.

Jenkins, Louis. *Nice Fish: New and Selected Prose Poems*. Duluth, MN: Holy Cow! Press, 1996.

Johnson, Peter. *Eduardo & "I"*. Buffalo, NY: White Pine Press, 2006.

Johnson, Peter. *Miracles and Mortifications*. Buffalo, NY: White Pine Press, 2001.

Johnson, Peter. *Pretty Happy*. Buffalo, NY: White Pine Press, 1997.

Kafka, Franz. Ed. Max Brod. *The Blue Octavo Notebooks*. Cambridge, MA: Exact Change, 2004.

Kalamaras, George. *Even the Java Sparrows Call Your Hair*. Williamsburg, MA: Quale Press, 2004.

Kennedy, Christopher. *Trouble with the Machine*. Brooklyn, NY: Low Fidelity Press, 2003.

Keplinger, David. *The Prayers of Others*. Kalamazoo, MI: New Issues Press, 2006.

Kharms, Daniil. Trans. Matvei Yankelevich. *Today I Wrote Nothing: The Selected Writings of Daniil Kharms*. New York: The Overlook Press, 2009.

Kilwein Guevara, Maurice. *Autobiography of So-and-so: Poems in Prose*. Kalamazoo, MI: New Issues Press, 2001.

Klassnik, Rauan. *Holy Land*. Boston, MA: Black Ocean, 2008.

Koncel, Mary. *You Can Tell the Horse Anything*. North Adams, MA: Tupelo Press, 2003.

LaFemina, Gerry. *Zarathustra in Love*. Bay City, MI: Mayapple Press, 2001.

LaFemina, Gerry. *The Book of Clown Baby/Figures from the Big Time Circus Book*. Bay City, MI: Mayapple Press, 2007.

Lazar, David. *The Body of Brooklyn*. Iowa City, IA: University of Iowa Press, 2003.

Lispector, Clarice. Trans. Giovanni Pontiero. *Selected Cronicas: Essays*. New York: New Directions, 1996.

Long, Alexander. *Light Here, Light There*. Chattanooga, TN: C & R Press, 2009.

Marcus, Morton. *Moments without Names: New and Selected Prose Poems*. Buffalo, NY: White Pine Press, 2005.

Mark, Sabrina Orah. *The Babies*. Ardmore, PA: Saturnalia Books, 2004.

Mark, Sabrina Orah. *Tsim Tsum*. Ardmore, PA: Saturnalia Books, 2009.

McCain, Gillian. *Tilt*. Lenox, MA: Hard Press Editions, 1996.

McGookey, Kathleen. *Whatever Shines*. Buffalo, NY: White Pine Press, 2001.

McGrath, Campbell. *Heart of Anthracite*. Dover, UK: Stride, 2004.

McGrath, Campbell. *Road Atlas: Prose and Other Poems*. New York: Ecco Press, 2001.

Merwin, W.S. *The Book of Fables*. Port Townsend, WA: Copper Canyon Press, 2007.

Michaux, Henri. Trans. Richard Ellmann. *Selected Writings of Henri Michaux*. New York: New Directions, 1990.

Michaux, Henri. *Darkness Moves: An Henri Michaux Anthology, 1927-1984*. Berkeley, CA: University of California Press, 1997.

Milosz, Czeslaw. Trans. Robert Hass. *Road-side Dog*. New York: Farrar, Straus and Giroux, 1999.

Miltner, Robert. *A Box of Light: Prose Poems*. Johnstown, OH: Pudding House Press, 2002.

Mullen, Harryette. *Recyclopedia: Trimmings, S*PeRM**K*T, and Muse & Drudge*. Minneapolis, MN: Graywolf Press, 2006.

Newman, Amy. *fall*. Middletown, CT: Wesleyan, 2004.

Olsen, William. *Avenue of Vanishing*. Evanston, IL: TriQuarterly Books, 2007.

Pessoa, Fernando. Trans. Richard Zenith. *The Book of Disquiet*. New York: Penguin Classics, 2002.

Phillips, Jayne Anne. *Black Tickets: Stories*. New York: Vintage, 2001.

Ponge, Francis. *La parti pris des choses*. Paris: Bertrand Lacoste, 1994.

Ponge, Francis. Trans. Lane Dunlop. *Soap*. Stanford, CA: Stanford University Press, 1998.

Ponge, Francis. Trans. Lee Fahnestock. *The Nature of Things*. Brooklyn, NY: Red Dust, Inc., 1995.

Rankine, Claudia. *Don't Let Me Be Lonely: An American Lyric*. Minneapolis, MN: Graywolf Press, 2004.

Richardson, James. *Vectors: Aphorisms & Ten-Second Essays*. Keene, NY: Ausable Press, 2001.

Rimbaud, Arthur. Trans. Daniel Sloate. *Illuminations*. New York: New Directions, 1957.

Roberts, Andrew Michael. *Give Up*. Grafton, VT: Tarpaulin Sky Press, 2006.

Robins, Michael. *The Next Settlement*. Denton, TX: University of North Texas Press, 2007.

Roubaud, Jacques. Trans. Rosmarie Waldrop. *Some Thing Black*. Normal, IL: Dalkey Archive Press, 1999.

Ruefle, Mary. *The Most of It*. Seattle, WA: Wave Books, 2008.

Samyn, Mary Ann. *Inside the Yellow Dress*. Kalamazoo, MI: New Issues Press, 2001.

Scalapino, Leslie. *that they were at the beach*. Los Angeles, CA: Green Integer Books, 1992.

Seaton, Maureen. *Venus Examines Her Breast*. Pittsburgh, PA: Carnegie Mellon University Press, 2004.

Sebald, W.G. *After Nature*. New York: Modern Library, 2003.

Shapiro, Karl. *The Bourgeois Poet*. New York: Random House, 1964.

Shumate, David. *High Water Mark: Prose Poems*. Pittsburgh, PA: University of Pittsburgh Press, 2004.

Shumate, David. *The Floating Bridge: Prose Poems*. Pittsburgh, PA: University of Pittsburgh Press, 2008.

Siken, Richard. *Crush*. New Haven, CT: Yale University Press, 2005.

Simic, Charles. *Dime-Store Alchemy: The Art of Joseph Cornell*. New York: NYRB Classics, 2006.

Simic, Charles. *The World Doesn't End*. New York: Harcourt Brace & Company, 1989.

Skinner, Jeffrey. *Salt Water Amnesia*. Keene, NY: Ausable Press, 2005.

Stein, Gertrude. *Tender Buttons*. New York: Dover Publications, 1997.

Strand, Mark. *The Monument*. New York: Ecco Press, 1978.

Tate, James. *Selected Poems*. Middletown, CT: Wesleyan University Press, 1991.

Tost, Tony. *Invisible Bride*. Baton Rouge, LA: Louisiana State University Press, 2004.

Waldie, D.J. *Holy Land: A Suburban Memoir*. New York: W.W. Norton, 2005.

Waldner, Liz. *A Point Is That Which Has No Part*. Iowa City, IA: University of Iowa Press, 2000.

Waldrep, G.C. *Archicembalo*. North Adams, MA: Tupelo Press, 2009.

Waldrop, Rosmarie. *Curves to the Apple*. New York: New Directions, 2006.

Wallace, Mark. *Temporary Worker Rides a Subway*. Los Angeles, CA: Green Integer Books, 2004.

White, Allison Benis. *Self-Portrait with Crayon*. Cleveland, OH: Cleveland State University Poetry Center, 2009.

Williams, William Carlos. *Kora in Hell*. San Francisco, CA: City Lights, 1957.

Wright, C.D. *Deepstep Come Shining*. Port Townsend, WA: Copper Canyon Press, 1998.

Young, Gary. *No Other Life*. Berkeley, CA: Heyday Books, 2005.

CREDITS

Nin Andrews: "Crossing" from *Sleeping with Houdini*. Copyright © 2007 by Nin Andrews. Used with the permission of BOA Editions, Ltd., www.boaeditions.org.; "Simplicity" by Henri Michaux, translated by Nin Andrews, from *Someone Wants to Steal My Name*, (Cleveland State University Poetry Center, 2004); "About the Dead" first appeared in *Notre Dame Review*. Reprinted by permission of the author.

Joe Bonomo: "You wish that the book were titled EMPATHY in a language that you knew," from *Installations* by Joe Bonomo, copyright © 2008 by Joe Bonomo. Used by permission of Penguin, a division of Penguin Group (USA) Inc.; "After Serving" first appeared in *Poetry Northwest*, 1998. Reprinted by permission of the author.

John Bradley: "I Shall Be Released" first appeared in *Quick Fiction*. Reprinted by permission of the author; "Parable of the Astral Wheel" first appeared in *Luna*. Reprinted by permission of the author.

Brigitte Byrd: "(How to Sink the Surface)" and "(After Contemplating Wintering in Water)" from *Song of a Living Room* by Brigitte Byrd, Ahsahta Press, 2009. Reprinted with permission of Ahsahta Press.

Maxine Chernoff: "Form and Function: Language in a Double World" appeared in *Bear Flag Republic*, edited by Christopher Buckley and Gary Young, Greenhouse Review Press/Alcatraz Editions, 2008. Used by permission of Greenhouse Review Press; "Subtraction" first appeared in *Leap Year Day*, Jensen-Daniels Press, 1991, and in *Utopia TV Store*, Yellow Press, 1979. Reprinted by permission of the author; "Heavenly Bodies" appeared in *World*, Salt Publishing, 2001, and *Evolution of the Bridge*, Salt Publishing, 2003. Reprinted by permission of the author; "He Picked up His Pen in Her Defense" from *The Turning*, Apogee Press, 2008. Reprinted by permission of the author.

David Daniel: "Paint" and "Hotel" from *Seven-Star Bird*. Copyright © 2003 by David Daniel. Reprinted with the permission of Graywolf Press, www.graywolfpress.org.

Denise Duhamel: "Embarazar" and "Napping on the Afternoon of My 39th Birthday" from *Two and Two*, by Denise Duhamel, copyright © 2005. Reprinted by permission of the University of Pittsburgh Press; Quoted in Duhamel's essay: "Happy" from *Sweethearts* by Jayne Anne Phillips, Truck Press, 1976. Reprinted with permission of Jayne Anne Phillips.

Nancy Eimers: "I Find in a Boke Compiled to this Matere an Old Histoire" and "Photograph of a Young Girl, 1941" from *A Grammar to Waking*. Copyright © 2005 by Nancy Eimers. Reprinted with the permission of Carnegie Mellon University Press, www.cmu.edu/universitypress.

Beckian Fritz Goldberg: "I Wish I Were Mexico" first appeared in *Hayden's Ferry Review*; reprinted by permission of the author; "He Said Discipline Is the Highest Form of Love" first appeared in *Blackbird*; reprinted by permission of the author.

Ray Gonzalez: "No Tongue in Cheek: The True Frame of the Prose Poem" from *Truth in Nonfiction* (where it appeared as "The True Frame of the Prose Poem"), University of Iowa Press, 2008. Reprinted with permission of University of Iowa Press; "Sticky Monkey Flowers" from *Human Crying Daisies* by Ray Gonzalez, Red Hen Press, 2003. Reprinted by permission of the author; Quoted in Gonzalez's essay: "Wall" from *The Collected Poems: 1956-1998* by Zbigniew Herbert Translated & Edited by Alissa Valles*. Copyright © 2007 the Estate of Zbigniew Herbert. Translation copyright © 2007 by Alissa Valles. Introduction copyright © 2007 by Adam Zagajewski. Reprinted by permission of HarperCollins Publishers With Additional Translations by Czeslaw Milosz and Peter Dale Scott.

Kevin Griffith: "Furnace" and "National Poetry Month" from *Denmark, Kangaroo, Orange* by Kevin Griffith, Pearl Editions, 2008. Reprinted by permission of the author.

Carol Guess: "The Belltown Angel" first appeared in *Bat City Review*; reprinted by permission of the author.

James Harms: "'Goodtime Jesus' and Other Sort-of Prose Poems" appeared in *Bear Flag Republic*, edited by Christopher Buckley and Gary Young, Greenhouse Review Press/Alcatraz Editions, 2008. Used by permission of Greenhouse Review Press; "Union Station, Los Angeles (The Reagan Years)" from *Freeways and Aqueducts*. Copyright © 2004 by James Harms. Reprinted with the permission of Carnegie Mellon University Press, www.cmu.edu/universitypress.

Tung-Hui Hu: "Lisboa, 1755" and "Five Dollars" from *Mine*. Copyright © 2007 by Tung-Hui Hu. Reprinted with permission of Copper Canyon Press, www.coppercanyon-press.org.

Christopher Kennedy: "Encouragement for a Man Falling to His Death" from *Encouragement for a Man Falling to His Death*. Copyright © 2007 by Christopher Kennedy. Reprinted with the permission of BOA Editions, Ltd., www.boaeditions.org; "Personality Quiz" from *Nietzsche's Horse* by Christopher Kennedy, Mitki/Mitki Press, 2003. Reprinted by permission of the author.

David Keplinger: "I stood too close…" and "I was a fabulous…" from *The Prayers of Others* by David Keplinger, New Issues Press, 2006. Used by permission of New Issues Press. Quoted in Keplinger's essay: Matthew Rohrer, "Disquisition on Trees" from *A Green Light*. Copyright © 2004 by Matthew Rohrer. Published by Verse Press. Reprinted with permission of Wave Books and the author.

Maurice Kilwein Guevara: "Soup for an Oligarch" and "the other word for thesaurus" from *Poema* by Maurice Kilwein Guevara, copyright © 2009 Maurice Kilwein Guevara. Reprinted by permission of the University of Arizona Press.

Gerry LaFemina: "Existentialism" first appeared in *Nimrod*, Spring/Summer 2005. Reprinted by permission of the author; "Feast" by Ali Yuce, translated by Sinan Toprak and Gerry LaFemina, from *Voice Lock Puppet*, Washington, DC: Orchises Press 2002. Used by permission of Gerry LaFemina; Quoted in LaFemina's essay: "The Two Brothers" from *Standing Room* by Gian Lombardo. Used with permission of Gian Lombardo. *Standing Room*, Baltimore: Dolphin Moon Press, 1989.

David Lazar: "Dark Lady of the Movies" and "Good Idea" from *Powder Town* by David Lazar, Pecan Grove Press, 1998. Reprinted by permission of the author.

Alexander Long: "Noise" first appeared in *Third Coast*. Reprinted by permission of the author; "Mediation on a Suicide" first appeared in *The Prose Poem: An International Journal*. Reprinted by permission of the author.

Robert Miltner: "Schism" first appeared as a broadside in *Bottle of Smoke*, 2007. Reprinted by permission of the author; "You Know What They Say about Pears" first appeared in *Artful Dodge*, 2003. Reprinted by permission of the author.

Amy Newman: "Dear Editor 18 January" first appeared in *Seneca Review*. Reprinted by permission of the author; "Dear Editor 30 October" first appeared in */nor* under a different title. Reprinted with permission of the author.

Andrew Michael Roberts: "Signs of Life" from *Give Up* by Andrew Michael Roberts, Tarpaulin Sky Press, 2006. Reprinted with permission of Tarpaulin Sky Press and the author; "Love Crushed Us with Its Big Death Truck" first appeared in *Harpur Palate*, 2006. Reprinted by permission of the author; "The Legacy" first appeared in *Margie*, Volume 5. Reprinted by permission of the author. Quoted in Roberts' essay: "Independence Day" by Sherman Alexie. Reprinted from *The Business of Fancydancing* © 1992 by Sherman Alexie, by permission of Hanging Loose Press.

Michael Robins: "Still Life with Steam Engine" and "Still Life with Gravestone" from *The Next Settlement* by Michael Robins, University of North Texas Press, 2007. Used by permission of University of North Texas Press.

Mary Ann Samyn: "From the Little Book of Female Mystics" from *Beauty Breaks In* by Mary Ann Samyn, New Issues Press, 2009. Used by permission of New Issues Press; "Wish You Were Here" from *Inside the Yellow Dress* by Mary Ann Samyn, New Issues Press, 2001. Used by permission of New Issues Press.

Maureen Seaton: "Ice" from *Little Ice Age* by Maureen Seaton, Invisible Cities Press, 2001. Used by permission of Invisible Cities Press; "The Realm of the Wide" from *Venus Examines Her Breast*. Copyright © 2004 Maureen Seaton. Reprinted with the permission of Carnegie Mellon University Press, www.cmu.edu/universitypress.

David Shumate: "Taking the Psychological Test" first appeared in *Poetry East*, Spring 2009. Reprinted by permission of the author; "After They Plundered the Language" first appeared in *Flying Island*, May 2008. Reprinted by permission of the author.

Jeffrey Skinner: "Many Worlds" and "The Experiment" from *Salt Water Amnesia*. Copyright © 2005 by Jeffrey Skinner. Reprinted with permission of Copper Canyon Press, www.coppercanyonpress.org.

Gary Young: "The Unbroken Line" first appeared in *Bear Flag Republic*, edited by Christopher Buckley and Gary Young, Greenhouse Review Press/Alcatraz Editions, 2008. Reprinted by permission of the author; "I couldn't find the mushrooms" from *Pleasure*, by Gary Young, Heyday Books, 2006. Reprinted by permission of Heyday Books; "The earth submits to seasonal drift" first appeared in *The Normal School*. Reprinted by permission of the author.

ACKNOWLEDGMENTS

In addition to the sources fully cited after and within individual essays and the introduction, the following sources were referenced:

Atwood, Margaret. "Making Poison." *Murder in the Dark*. Toronto, ON: Coach House, 1983. Print.

Baudelaire, Charles. *Paris Spleen*. Trans. Louise Varése. New York: New Directions, 1970. Print.

Benedikt, Michael. *The Prose Poem: An International Anthology*. New York: Laurel Dell, 1976. Print.

Bertrand, Aloysius. *Flemish School, Old Paris, & Night & Its Spells*. Trans. Gian Lombardo. Florence, MA: Quale Press, 2000. Print.

Blake, William. "The Marriage of Heaven and Hell." *The Complete Poetry and Prose of William Blake*. New York: Doubleday, 1998. Print.

Bryson, Norman. *Looking at the Overlooked: Four Essays on Still Life Painting*. London: Reaktion Books, 2004. Print.

Carson, Anne. "On Orchids." *Plainwater*. New York: Knopf, 1995. Print.

Conrad, Joseph. *The Nigger of the "Narcissus."* New York: WW Norton, 1979. Print.

Delville, Michel. *The American Prose Poem: Poetic Form and the Boundaries of Genre*. Gainesville, FL: University Press of Florida, 1998. Print.

Duhamel, Denise. "Response & Bio." *Double Room* 1 (2002/2003). Web. 22 Dec. 2009.

Edson, Russell. "Portrait of the Writer as a Fat Man: Some Subjective Ideas on the Care and Feeding of Prose Poems." *A Field Guide to Contemporary Poetry and Poetics*. Eds. Stuart Friebert and David Young. New York: Longman, 1980. Print.

Edson, Russell. *The Tunnel: Selected Poems*. Oberlin, OH: Oberlin College Press, 1994. Print.

"Fu (Poetry)." *Wikipedia*. Wikimedia, n.d. Web. 28 December, 2009.

Hass, Robert. "An Informal Occasion with Robert Hass." *Iowa Review* 21:3 (1991): 126-45. Print.

Hirshfield, Jane. *Nine Gates: Entering the Mind of Poetry*. New York: HarperCollins, 1997. Print.

Iglesias, Holly. *Boxing Inside the Box: Women's Prose Poetry*. Williamsburg, MA: Quale Press, 2004. Print.

Kundera, Milan. *The Unbearable Lightness of Being*. Trans. Michael Henry Hein. New York: Harper & Row, 1984. Print.

Lehman, David. "Introduction." *Great American Prose Poems: From Poe to the Present*. New York: Scribner, 2003. Print.

Luria, A.R. *Language and Cognition*. New York: Wiley, 1982. Print.

"Mallarmé, Stephan." Answers.com. n.d. Web. 28 December 2009.

Maloney, Dennis, ed. *Dreaming the Miracle: Three French Prose Poets: Max Jacob, Jean Follain, and Francis Ponge*. Buffalo, NY: White Pine Press, 2002. Print.

McGrath, Campbell. "Manitoba." *Road Atlas*. New York: Ecco Press, 1999. Print.

McGrath, Campbell. "The Prose Poem." *Road Atlas*. New York: Ecco Press, 1999. Print.

Merwin, W.S. *The Miner's Pale Children*. New York: Atheneum, 1970. Print.

O'Hara, Frank. "Steps." *Collected Poems*. Berkeley, CA: University of California Press, 1995. Print.

Pater, Walter. *Renaissance*. Mineola, NY: Dover, 2005. Print.

Ponge, Francis. "Memorandum." *Selected Poems*. Trans. C.K. Williams. Winston-Salem, NC: Wake Forest University Press, 1994. Print.

Richardson, James. *Interglacial: New and Selected Poems & Aphorisms*. Keene, NY: Ausable Press, 2004. Print.

Shapiro, Karl. *The Bourgeois Poet*. New York: Random House, 1964. Print.

Sharp, William. *Vistas: The Gypsy Christ, and Other Prose Imaginings*. Ann Arbor, MI: University of Michigan Press, 2009. Print.

Tate, James. Interview by Charles Simic. "The Art of Poetry No. 92." *The Paris Review* Summer 2006. Print.

Young, Stephen. *The Philosophy Gym*. New York: St. Martin's Press, 2003. Print.

This book would not have been possible without the guidance and enthusiasm of David Hassler, who answered questions, presented recommendations for improvement, and suggested publishers while this project was just an idea. We'd also like to thank the editors who read and commented on this project in its earliest stages: Holly Carver and Joseph Parsons at University of Iowa Press, Peter Conners at BOA Editions, Ltd., and Sarah Gorham at Sarabande Books. Thanks also to our contributors for taking on our requests and suggestions, for being flexible while various aspects of this project have fluctuated over the last few years, and for writing enlightening things about prose poetry. Our highest thanks goes to our editors, Abigail Beckel and Kathleen Rooney of Rose Metal Press—thank you for probing and refining many of our ideas for this book, for challenging our perceptions of ourselves as editors and writers, for being watchful, patient, and persistent, and for believing in this book as much as we do.

Dan would like to thank his wife Amanda for her steadfast support of this project and for her incredible patience over the last four years. He would also like to thank his family and friends for their belief and support.

Gary would like to thank his friends and family for their support, encouragement, and enthusiasm during the course of this project, namely Michael Cherry, Adam Clay, Dennis McDowell, Keith Montesano, Julie Platt, Chad Sweeney, and others he has possibly forgotten. A special thanks to his wife, Mandy, and his son, Auden: Thanks for everything and everything else.

ABOUT THE EDITORS

Gary L. McDowell was born and raised in suburban Chicago. He earned a BA in English from Northern Illinois University and an MFA in Poetry from Bowling Green State University. He currently teaches writing at Western Michigan University where he is studying for his PhD in Contemporary Poetics and American Literature. His first collection of poems, *American Amen*, won the 2009 Orphic Prize and will appear in late 2010 from Dream Horse Press. He is also the author of two chapbooks, *They Speak of Fruit* (Cooper Dillon, 2009) and *The Blueprint* (Pudding House, 2005). His poems have been nominated several times for a Pushcart Prize, and have appeared in various literary journals, including *Colorado Review, Indiana Review, The Laurel Review, New England Review, Ninth Letter, Poetry Daily*, and *Quarterly West*. He lives in Kalamazoo, Michigan with his wife and their young son, Auden.

F. Daniel Rzicznek earned a BA in English from Kent State University and an MFA in Creative Writing from Bowling Green State University. His chapbook of prose poems, *Cloud Tablets*, was published by Kent State University Press in 2006 as part of the Wick Poetry Chapbook Series. In 2007, he won the May Swenson Poetry Award for his debut full-length collection, *Neck of the World*. In 2009 his second collection of poems, *Divination Machine*, appeared on the Free Verse Editions imprint of Parlor Press. His individual poems have been published in *The New Republic, Boston Review, Orion, Shenandoah, AGNI, The Iowa Review*, and *Mississippi Review*, among others, and have been nominated three times for the Pushcart Prize. Currently he teaches English composition and creative writing at Bowling Green State University. He lives with his wife, the writer Amanda McGuire, in Bowling Green, Ohio.

A NOTE ABOUT THE TYPE

The main text of this book is set in Robert Slimbach's Utopia. Released in 1989, Utopia was one of the first original digital text families introduced to the Adobe Originals program. As book designers began to transition to using the computer for design, the demand for high-quality digital type-faces followed. Adobe released fonts from their Originals collection to meet this demand. Utopia's balanced stroke and varied character weights make it a highly legible and versatile type family. Utopia is not without touches of elegance evident in carefully crafted letterforms.

The display text throughout this book showcases Avenir. Swiss design-er Adrian Frutiger created Avenir in 1988 for the Linotype type foundry. French for "future," Avenir most resembles, and is in fact inspired by, Paul Renner's geometric sans Futura; however Frutiger softened some of the sharp edges that pervade Futura's letterforms. The result is a more organ-ic and relaxed typeface that is stylistically fresh and yet still durable.

Sprinkled throughout the text is a dingbat that comes from the Kepler Ornaments family.

– Rebecca Saraceno